A level in a week

Andrew Hoskins, Abbey Tutorial College
Series editor: Kevin Byrne

C000080845

Where to find the information you need

Letts Educational
Aldine Place
London W12 8AW
Tel: 0181 740 2266
Fax: 0181 743 8541
e-mail: mail@lettsed.co.uk
website: http://www.lettsed.co.uk

First published 1999

British Library Cataloguing in Publication Data
A CIP record for this book is available from the British Library.

ISBN 1 85758 9335

Editorial, design and production by Hart McLeod, Cambridge

Printed in Great Britain by Ashford Colour Press

Letts Educational is the trading name of BPP (Letts Educational) Ltd

Mass media

Test your knowledge

20 minutes

1 Define (a) mass media and (b) mass communication.

2 Distinguish between 'old' or traditional forms of media and 'new' media.

3 'The medium is the message' and the 'global village' were influential phrases in the study of the nature of the relationship between technology and mass media used by _____ _____ in the 1950s and 1960s.

4 There is some debate over whether the media actually create meaning or not. In this sense do the media construct or represent reality, or do they merely reflect it? For example, some influential empirical work into the nature of news content on British television was undertaken by the _____ _____ _____ _____, and was first published as *Bad News* (1976).

5 (a) Consideration of media effects is usually focused on the nature and response of the audience. Phases in audience research began with assumptions based on a _____ _____ model of messages acting directly on a _____ mass audience.

   (b) The 1970s saw the rise of the notion of an active audience based on how the audience used media messages and sought escapism. This approach became known as the _____ and _____ perspective.

6 Influence of the mass media: name four perspectives on the relationship between media and society.

7 The two principal trends of media ownership are _____ and _____.

Answers

1 (a) communication industries and technologies themselves (b) transmission and reception of information and entertainment via the mass media across time and space **2** traditional media: TV, radio, cinema, magazines, newspapers, books, billboards, etc.; 'new': computers, the Internet, digital TV/radio, multi-media **3** Marshall McLuhan **4** Glasgow University Media Group **5** (a) 'hypodermic syringe', passive (b) 'uses and gratifications' **6** (a) liberal pluralism, liberal paternalism, free market liberalism or 'new right', Marxist **7** concentration and conglomeration

✔ *If you got them all right, skip to page 6*

Mass media

Improve your knowledge

1 Perspectives on the media can be misleading when linked to meanings of the notion of **mass**. For example: the inhabiting of one world, undifferentiated or homogeneous, leads to assumptions about the nature of the **mass media** and a **mass audience**, that is to say, one consisting of few sources, many receivers and with limited opportunity for feedback.

The mass media as a plural term is often treated as a uniform and singular entity, leading to simplistic theoretical **models** of the nature of communication, i.e. of senders, receivers, the 'message' or 'text' itself and the channels of communication between them. Instead of mass media, think of the **media mix**, consisting of **multiple** senders and receivers sending/receiving multiple messages via multiple channels, i.e. a potentially very complex picture.

many simultaneous senders, receivers and messages

2 There has been a **communications explosion** in recent years, fuelled by technological transformation, e.g. satellite communications, the digitisation of data (digital signals rather than analogue) giving rise to the advent of digital television and radio. Superfast channels of communication, such as fibre optics, allow multiple signals to be transmitted along single lines. These technological advances give access to many more channels which, advocates claim, improve media **choice**. Also, vast improvements in the power and speed of computers have been matched by declining production costs.

more technology = more choice?

3 Marshall McLuhan argued that the **nature** of the communication is more important than the **content**. Although writing over three decades ago, McLuhan placed importance on how we **interact** with the media. The new media have collapsed time and distance and connected places/people/audiences as part of a process called **globalisation**. However, although the satellite and digital technology of today give the media a potentially new global **reach**, McLuhan was not particularly critical of those who controlled the media, and those in the underdeveloped world have still remained as 'poor' neighbours in the global village. Furthermore, global media messages or **texts** are not universal experiences. Television texts have more than one meaning – they are **polysemic** (Fiske, 1989). Similarly, there is resistance in their interpretation by **heterogeneous** audiences.

electronic global reach = 'the extensions of man' (McLuhan)

multiple 'readings' of texts

4 The Glasgow University Media Group remit of enquiry into the news is summed up by Eldridge (1993) in terms of: '**objectivity, impartiality and neutrality**'. Their research essentially involved looking at a system of ideas expressed through communication – also known as **ideology**.

Their study of industrial relations on television news is important in that it was the first substantial empirical study of this kind, and is still used as a benchmark today. They used quantitative analysis of data, comparing TV news reports. Their interpretations were informed by a Marxist approach through their class-based analysis and an Interactionist approach through the comparison of the sources and location of reports, and the language used to represent management and workers. Their main findings were that news was typically presented in a biased fashion. The effects of strikes were more likely to be reported than their causes. Industrial relations were portrayed as disruptive.

quantitative method

news bias

Harrison (1985) argued GUMG research was politically motivated, over an atypical period of study and misrepresented ITN (although Harrison himself was partly sponsored by ITN). Anderson and Sharrock argued GUMG treated the audience as 'passive dopes', unable to interpret or 'filter' out bias in the presentation of news.

5 Technological and cultural changes have helped to transform the sociological 'view' of the audience. Also, it is important not to assume that the audience is only a televisual one. For example, Abercrombie and Longhurst (1998) define three types of audience (not necessarily exclusive of each other), namely, a **simple**, **mass** and **diffused** audience.

- Simple – their label for those gathered usually in a public space involving a certain immediacy (e.g. attending concerts, football matches, political meetings etc.).
- Mass – is the audience of mass communication (e.g. TV, radio, music on CD etc.).
- Diffused – describes the nature of the audience–media relationship in our 'media drenched society' in which we 'become audiences all the time'. That is, the amount of time we spend consuming media at home (private spaces) and in public leads Abercrombie and Longhurst to argue that the media are actually **constitutive** of everyday life. One can compare this with the approach of John Thompson (1995) who defines 'mediated-quasi interaction' as a form of communication that is an 'ongoing process' where media messages are received, discussed, retold, etc. and this is how they enter into our daily experience. So, through recognising the complexities of the nature of the audience today, 'reading' the audience has become a more complex task.

6 (a) **Liberal pluralism** is the most popular perspective linking freedom in the media and political freedom with that of the economy and market. For society to be democratic, individuals and groups must be free to exert influence through and upon the media. The audience have access to the media to mould and shape output by virtue of their feedback. For example Whale (1987) argues that newspaper readers have more influence than proprietors and advocates an entirely *laissez-faire* approach.

(b) **Liberal Paternalists** believe the media should also reflect and maintain high cultural goals, standards and quality. This approach expects some degree of state intervention through regulation to maintain standards and has been particularly supportive of public broadcasting, i.e. recent legislation, the 1990 Broadcasting Act.

(c) The **New Right** reject those groups attempting to impose 'quality' as interfering with freedom and propose instead a **populist** approach involving the free market of a wholly private media open to competition and consumer demand.

(d) A **Marxist** approach argues that the ideas and values which are favourable to capitalist society are those dominant in the media. Marxists argue that the capitalist or private control of the media reproduces and reinforces capitalist ideology. Some Liberal Pluralists counter this argument in claiming that a 'managerial revolution' has taken place (Burnham, 1943). However, contemporary Marxists Murdock and Golding (1977) argue that concentration and conglomeration have led to more control in the hands of owners. Furthermore, they claim that even if media organisations were run by managers accountable to shareholders and the general public, they are still nonetheless run for **profit**.

media economy

7 **Concentration** is the process whereby business in one area, e.g. media, merges to create a concentration of ownership/control/power in fewer hands, for example, in the national press. **Conglomeration** occurs when a company takes over another or others. This form of expansion is not limited by national boundaries (i.e. **transnational** companies) or to same-product take-overs. In the global market there is an emphasis on diversification. Often ownership of large firms is concentrated in the hands of mass shareholding individuals. Rupert Murdoch is perhaps the best known media entrepreneur or media **mogul** with his control of News International Corporation which owns a number of national daily and Sunday newspapers in Britain along with other publications. Other News International holdings include Sky television, HarperCollins (book publisher), the news organisation Reuters, and Reed and Pearson – two other large media groups.

global economy

Murdoch's *Sun* newspaper (the national daily with the largest circulation – in excess of three million) is perhaps the most notorious title within this group. More recently the relationship between Murdoch and the new Labour government has been placed under some scrutiny in relation to the nature and extent of the influence of Murdoch over government (for example, in respect of the issue of Britain's closer European integration).

who sets the political agenda?

✓ *Now learn how to use your knowledge*

Mass media

Use your knowledge

60 minutes

Hints

1 In what ways do mass messages, products or brands survive across a spectrum of the media mix? For example, think of the global branding of consumption in the form of soft drinks, film or pop stars.

image saturation?

2 How useful is the comparison between 'old' and 'new' media? Are the new media ushering us into a distinct new historical period or are we experiencing just 'more of the same' in terms of our living in a media-saturated world? Describe a post-modern explanation of these changes.

what is a 'post-modern' experience like?

3 When new technology extends the global reach of the media relatively cheaply (e.g. the clockwork radio in Africa), can we then speak of the beginnings of a 'global media culture'? What are the 'mixed messages' in terms of the senders and receivers of the global media?

think here in terms of advertising and consumption

4 There are broadly two notions of ideology. One is the neutral conception whereby dominant ideas are communicated without being deliberately misleading or part of the interests of a particular group. The other is the exercise of **symbolic power** (Thompson, 1995), whereby the dominance of certain groups is disguised or justified.

(a) How has research by the Glasgow University Media Group and others helped to differentiate between these types of ideology?

(b) Could the GUMG approach be used in the television news environment of today?

(c) Is news in Britain free from bias? Could it ever be?

think how news is routinely presented

5 According to Abercrombie and Longhurst, the media are constitutive of our everyday lives.

(a) Make a list of the ways in which you consider yourself to be part of a 'mass' audience.

(b) Given the recent technological changes and the advent of a 'global media age', are we, as an audience, more or less well informed?

where and from whom do you get your news?

6 Assess critically different perspectives on the influence of the media in relation to the following recent developments:

(a) The deregulation of the airwaves by the 1990 Broadcasting Act, the mass increase in the availability of radio and television channels, and the accusation that there has been a 'dumbing down' in the content of programmes as a result.

(b) The public backlash against the media following the death of Diana, Princess of Wales.

(c) New methods of organising 'resistance' to the media based on the cheap electronic storage, retrieval and movement of information. For example, Murdoch and Golding (1977) describe an 'alternative radical media scope'.

7 Examine the relationship between media ownership and editorial control. To what extent are newspaper editors, for example, independent of their owners? Do owners directly control the media or do they not need to intervene in editorial decisions because they share the same social values as those who produce printed titles and programmes on TV and radio?

what influence can 'ownership' buy?

To what extent do you agree with Abercrombie, Ward et al. (1994) who suggest that 'owners, producers and audiences are bound together in a set of social values that are continually reinforced in media content'?

Answers on page 61

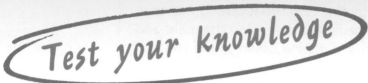

Culture and identity

Test your knowledge

20 minutes

1 Culture is a way of life. It is constructed through the language, beliefs, norms, values, traditions, customs and habits of a _____ group. Its transmission is _____ (in the background or subconscious). At the same time culture is something that is acquired or _____ through a process of _____ and helps form individual and collective _____.

2 The concept of a mass or _____ culture is largely a term used critically and developed in the 1920s and 1930s to describe in part the effects of the developing mass media. The 'critical theory' of the _____ _____ critiqued the 'mass deception' in the areas of entertainment, leisure, commerce and advertising through the mass media, which, together, Adorno and Horkheimer refer to as the _____ _____. Marcuse argued that the effects of mass culture resulted in a 'one-dimensional' American man. This perspective views the mass media as repressive and serving to _____ capitalism through the advance of mass culture.

3 Bourdieu in *Distinction* (1984) focuses on the notion of cultural reproduction and in particular, how middle and working class cultures are reproduced. For Bourdieu, _____ is the cultural background, the language, style and values that form cultural identity.

4 _____ is central to culture, for without it culture would cease to exist. Fiske provides a general definition of communication as 'social interaction through messages'. One perspective on how we come to recognise and understand culture is that of _____ (a term made popular by Lévi-Strauss).

5 The development of new technologies which permitted the rise of a _____ _____, and so a mass culture, from the second half of the nineteenth century is based on the phenomenon of modernism. The phase or period following that of modernism, marking a definitive change in the nature of art, culture, self and society, is known as _____.

Answers

5 mass market, post-modernism
4 communication, structuralism
3 habitus
2 standardised, Frankfurt School, culture industry, legitimise
1 social, tacit, learnt, socialisation, identity

If you got them all right, skip to page 14

Culture and identity

Improve your knowledge

30 minutes

1 Culture operates at many different and distinct levels:

- global
- national
- regional
- local.

There are cultures of religion, race or ethnicity, age, gender and class.

Popular culture is linked to a change in taste and in **patterns of consumption** that took off largely after the Second World War with the arrival of American and continental styles, fashion, film and music etc. in Britain. Hebdige (1981) points to the rise in the availability of consumer goods and the dramatic increase in the scale of working-class expenditure on leisure between the 1930s and 1960s. Popular culture is, in part, a **historical development** from folk culture.

Folk culture is associated with the lower classes who inhabited the public spaces of pre-modern societies (churches, pubs etc.). This was a kind of spontaneous and 'authentic' culture. The higher classes more typically inhabited the private space of the domestic sphere (**élite culture**). The distinction between folk and élite culture (largely based on class) was replaced with the modern distinction between popular and high culture.

High culture was perceived as the culture of the élite, for example, what counts as a 'good' cultural experience.

A critique of the distinction between popular and high culture is that it is oversimplified. For example, audiences of popular culture have been characterised as passive and powerless to resist, against the notion of audiences of high culture being active and engaging.

popular vs. high

The dilution of high culture by popular culture is seen as part of the move to a **three-minute culture**, where previously 'high' forms of art, literature, music etc. are 'packaged' into a more easily digestible form to appeal to a wider audience. This has even led to the criticism that three minutes is the average attention span of the popular consumer, i.e. there is little depth or meaning to their understanding.

popular = superficial?

Popular culture is often viewed as **commodified culture**, for example, Giner (1976) argues, 'Culture is now . . . only a commodity to be sold to as broad an audience as possible. In fact the audience has also changed for it is now a mass of prospective customers'.

an economy of culture?

A **sub-culture** is the culture of a social group that is distinct from, although related to, the dominant culture of a society. This concept is often related to **oppositional** elements to the dominant culture and to the emergence of youth as a market of consumption.

2 The debate concerning the nature of 'mass society' and hostility towards its development began in the early twentieth century. Lévi-Strauss, for example, warned of the 'evils' of mass society, claiming that the standards and quality of life were being 'levelled down' with the standardising of culture. This he considered to be putting 'at risk' the values of élite culture. 1930s poetry also reflected this view and claimed that a 'debased' popular culture had been produced (e.g. Betjeman).

The Frankfurt School study is an examination of **cultural stratification**. Swingewood (1977), however, argues that 'consumer capitalism' does not create a vast, homogeneous mass. Rather, it 'generates different levels of taste, different audiences and consumers. Culture is stratified, its consumption differentiated'. Similarly, Fiske (1989) argues that, 'a homogeneous, externally produced culture cannot be sold ready-made to the masses . . . Nor do the people behave or act like the masses . . . Popular culture is made by the people, not produced by the culture industry'.

'active' model

This positive perspective of mass culture can be broadly described as one of **cultural pluralism**. Popular culture is seen to fulfil a need of genuine taste in post-industrial society where people have greater freedom and choice. Shils, for example, characterises mass society as the **integration** of the mass of the population into society.

3 **Habitus**, for Bourdieu, links the culture of a society with the structuring of social relationships. He argues that those who possess **cultural capital,** in that they share the values, beliefs and outlook of, for example, the educational system, will perform well within that system. Working-class children are therefore disadvantaged in what Bourdieu perceives to be a middle-class educational system, i.e. they suffer a **cultural deficit.**

For Bourdieu, cultural goods are a marker of class. That is, our consumption of goods, of cultural products, in society is linked to their role as **markers**. Particular tastes, consumption preferences and lifestyles are associated with specific occupational and class groups. In capitalist societies there is an 'endless struggle' to obtain 'positional goods' that define social status (Hirsch, 1976).

you are what you eat/wear/drive

Following on from Bourdieu, Featherstone (1995) argues that a person's origins and path through life are betrayed by the means of body shape, size, weight, walk, way of speaking etc. So, 'culture is incorporated, and it is not just a question of what clothes are worn but of how they are worn'. This perspective on the production of culture, Featherstone calls a **'mode of consumption'** approach. So-called 'designer' clothes are now sold with labels sewn on the outside of garments – the **brand names** have become part of the fashion. In 1998, some supermarkets imported designer goods from outside the UK (where these clothes are sold more cheaply) to sell them at discounted prices. A number of companies complained and won a European Court ruling against this practice of 'grey' imports. They complained that the reduction in the price to consumers devalued the image of their products, i.e. as exclusive and of 'high' monetary and therefore symbolic value.

meaning produced in context

4 Lévi-Strauss uses the metaphor of geology to help explain **Structuralism**. The layering of rock formations over time all appear unique but at the same time share characteristics with underlying elements with similar geological phenomena. Similarly, our experience of culture can be understood by examining the underlying patterns that are 'linked' to the surface. Saussure, through his science of signs and meanings (now called **Semiotics**), argued that it is not only speaking or writing that make meanings, but also the representations we attach to, or that come from, 'things'. This requires **shared recognition of difference**. For example, 'fashion' is a common recognition of certain clothes and styles 'of the moment' rather than the item being worn in itself. From a structuralist perspective then, meaning in culture, as in language, is a matter of **difference**.

structuralist theory – think layers

Structuralists have been criticised by **interpretative** sociology, a perspective which rather than seeking to 'uncover' structures and laws, instead uses **interpretation** as a method of understanding people's lives, cultures and societies. The anthropologist Geertz (1979), for example, argues 'Cultures and their members should be treated as gatherings of texts by researchers'.

Post-structuralist views focus on the nature of meaning again, but instead contend that there is no longer a closed system of meaning. There is a loss of certainty associated with this perspective, that meaning is no longer immediately 'readable' in the sign but is scattered or 'dispersed'. In these circumstances, problems arise for the nature of the self in respect of identity. The loosening of the bonds to culture and society (of shared meaning and recognition) leaves the self abandoned from the collective meaning previously acquired through the agencies of socialisation. Giddens (1991), for example, describes this gloomy outlook: 'The self in modern society is frail, brittle, fractured [and] fragmented'.

⇒ the 'schizoid'?

5 **Modernism** is often considered in relation to the production of culture and art and who has access to these. Benjamin, for example, argues that the 'experience' of a cultural form or piece of art was available only to the privileged – namely those who could afford it. But, the new technologies that enabled **mass reproduction** to take place allowed access to the many rather than the few. The 'bad' side of this process, for Benjamin, however, is that culture becomes commodified and commercialised, so the 'essence' of the creation is lost. Today, we have pop songs sampling classical music, or Manet postcards, for example. For Benjamin, the **aura**, the singularity, uniqueness and so authority of the work of art is lost. Scott Lash (1990) argues that modernist culture 'effectively destabilises bourgeois identity' and gives rise to the 'working class as a collective actor'. So, the identity shaped by the exclusive culture of the middle classes was weakened through its reproduction. At the same time, the working class took on a more coherent collective identity based on their shared experience of mass-produced and available cultural forms.

loss of the original

Post-modernism is characterised by a shift in cultural norms. If modern culture and identity can be characterised by coherence and 'the collective', then the **post**-modern experience is one of fragmentation, of a **plurality** of cultural forms. Jameson argues that since the 1960s the production of culture has actually been 'integrated into commodity production'. He links post-modernism with the 'cultural logic of late capitalism' where the rapid turnover of goods/fashion/culture is designed to fulfil the desire created by capitalism, in order to sustain its markets. He sees the erosion of the distinction between 'popular' and 'high' culture as a feature of post-modernism. He argues that television and a 'Reader's Digest' culture levels down or simplifies high culture to a level for mass consumption.

loss of certainty

'dumbing down'

At the same time there is a more positive view of post-modernism – that of the breaking down of previously restraining collective ties and instead advocating the celebration of a multiplicity of cultures, 'selves', and sexualities. The city is seen as a focal point for the celebration of the cosmopolitan and fluid and playful identities. Individual identity is also said to become 'decentered' or fragmented so that each of us has a multiplicity of 'selves' corresponding to the different fragments or roles that make up post-modern life.

more complex identities

✔ *Now learn how to use your knowledge*

Culture and identity

60 minutes

Hints

1 In 1990 Denscombe argued that there is 'little evidence that "high culture" is opening up to the working class . . . Opera, ballet, the theatre and art galleries remain largely the privilege of the well-educated and the well-off'.

question the assumption in these definitions

To what extent would you agree with this statement if applied to culture in Britain today?

2 Compare and contrast a cultural pluralist view of the development of 'mass culture' in Britain with a 'critical theory' perspective.

3 Bourdieu has been criticised for producing a 'deterministic' view of cultural reproduction. What does 'deterministic' mean in this context and to what extent would you say this is fair criticism of Bourdieu?

4 What are the weaknesses in a structuralist approach to the study of culture and identity, as viewed from an interpretivist perspective?

is identity predetermined?

5 'Post-modernism' is a term associated with the notion of the 'speeding up' and fragmentation of culture and identity, and the rapid turnover of fashion, styles or movements in the arts, for example.

To what extent would you agree that we are experiencing a loss of identity and culture in this so-called 'post-modern' realm?

think of your own self-conception of identity

What evidence is there to suggest that culture and identity are much more resilient and lasting than this account of post-modernism suggests?

Answers on page 64

Family

Test your knowledge

15 minutes

1 The type of family characterised by a decrease in the segregation of the roles of men and women was defined as the '_____ family' by _____ and _____ (1973).

2 A society's values, norms and beliefs are learnt by the individual through the process of _____. This process that occurs within the agency of the family can be characterised as the earliest form of social 'training' or _____ _____.

3 According to information from the 1996 General Household Survey there are now more single person households (_____%) than there are married and cohabiting couples with dependent children (_____%).

4 The family of today is in part moulded by a rise of _____ individualism. Intimate relations based on feelings, sexual attraction and a persistent association with the notion of _____ _____ are the modern basis of marriage.

Given though, that the great majority of people who get married do so between the ages of 25 and 35 (first time marriages), this seems to indicate that there is a 'generalised _____ pressure' (Luhmann 1986) to get married.

5 The functionalist Talcott Parsons (1959) characterised the nuclear family as being _____ and the ideal and typical family form of industrial society. Support for the general thesis of a move from extended to nuclear family structure came from _____ (1963), and _____ and _____ (1965). Similarly, _____ and _____ (1968) refer to the 'privatisation of family life'.

_____ and _____ (1962) identified a healthy extended family network in their study of working-class life in Bethnal Green in the 1950s.

Answers

1 symmetrical, Willmott, Young 2 socialisation, primary socialisation 3 27%, 25% 4 affective, romantic love, social 5 isolated, Goode, Rosser, Harris, Goldthorpe, Lockwood, Willmott, Young

If you got them all right, skip to page 20

Family

Improve your knowledge

30 minutes

1 A **Feminist** critique of the symmetrical family approach is that based on the notion of the **patriarchal** family. The family is part of the institutionalisation of the dominance of men over women through the **domestic mode of production** in the home but Marxist-Feminists relate this to wider capitalist relations of production.

One method of the assessment of the **domestic division of labour** is the measurement of time spent on household tasks, e.g. Oakley (1974) in a sample of urban housewives claims to have found an average of 70 hours of housework in 1950 compared to 77, in 1971.

time on housework

Gershuny (1992) drawing upon surveys from the 1970s and 1980s considers the 'dual-burden' hypothesis: as wives enter the job market they still carry the burden of domestic work. However, at the same time, men have begun to take on more household tasks.

two types of work

Delphy (1984) provides a **Feminist critique** of housework, or rather 'domestic work' (to include both paid and unpaid work) which, she argues, cannot be defined as a 'task' or series of tasks, rather it is 'a certain work relationship', a particular relationship of **production**.

A more recent Feminist perspective is provided by Cockburn and Ormrod (1993) who suggest that 'overall housework hours are remaining more or less constant but the **composition** of household work and responsibility is changing'. For example, in addition to 'routine' domestic work, there is the time involved in shopping (including travel) and childcare. The social prevalence of the single-parent household, and the assumption of the essentially unaided housewife has led to technological developments which cater for this model of the family. Technological (time-saving) advances, increased childcare provision and 24-hour opening perhaps raise expectations for the housewife to do more, rather than less.

redefining housework

16

2 **Functionalists** emphasise the role of the family in this process of the internalisation of norms etc. leading to

- value consensus
- conformity
- social order.

Marxists view these 'functions' in a negative light and argue that the working-class family is subordinated to the means of production under capitalism.

Marxist Feminists incorporate biological (sexual and reproductive) divisions, that is the domestic production of labour and motherhood, into a Marxist viewpoint. They view patriarchy as bound to or subject to capitalism. However, more recently, the feminists Delphy and Leonard (1992) describe Marxist-Feminists' analyses of the family as 'disastrous'. They argue that the Marxist-Feminist approach did not tackle middle-class family relations and was reluctant to criticise the patriarchal power of working-class men. Instead, Delphy and Leonard focus on: 'the practical, emotional, sexual, procreative and symbolic <u>work done by women for men</u> within family relationships' (1992, emphasis added).

structural and biological

in relation to men

3 There has been a gradual reduction in the average size of households in Britain from 2.91 in 1971 to 2.40 in 1995 (2.43 in 1996) for a number of factors:

- the rise in the proportion of **single-person households**
- a halving in the proportion of households comprising of five or more persons from 14% to 7%
- the **'ageing population'**
- an increase in the proportion of **lone-parent** families.
  (Source: 'Living in Britain: Preliminary results from the 1995 General Household Survey', 1996.)

diverse household forms

Increased rates of separation and divorce, unmarried mothers or the death of a spouse all affect the trend in the number of single-parent families. The **reconstituted** or **step** family is usually defined as one in which there is at least one dependent child from a former relationship of at least one of the 'new' partners. This definition, however, belies the potentially very complex experience of life in reconstituted families, given the effect of new and multiple familial ties.

diverse family structures

Ethnicity – about 50% of Afro-Caribbean families are single-parent and they tend to be mother-centred or **matrifocal**. This, however, does not preclude the social significance of other kin relationships within the same family. It is important not to make wider assumptions based on the different emphasis on familial relations. For example, extended familial networks tend to be more significant in West Indian groups, than in white families, in relation to the marital relationship.

4. Partners' **expectations** of marriage are often hard to fulfil, based on the **popular culture** and **commodification** of romantic love. At the same time, public **perception** of the ephemeral nature of marriage, that one in three marriages does not last 'for life' can be seen to affect couples' attitudes and approach to their own marriage. Partners can too easily interpret 'problems' at home as indicative of a breakdown in their marriage rather than as part of the 'ups and downs' of any intimate relationship. This effect has been enhanced with the lessening of the social **stigma** attached to **divorce** and **separation** (mostly since the 1969 Divorce Reform Act). This is part of what Luhmann (1986) refers to as a process of '**social regression**'. That is, under attack from numerous sources, marriage has been weakened and has lost some of its **socially binding** character in late modernity.

self-fulfilling prophecy

loosening of social ties

Christopher Lasch (1980) a radical American writer, argues that families are manipulated in the consumer society against a background of the 'culture of narcissism' where people enter into 'nonbinding commitments' and where lasting intimate relationships are increasingly difficult to achieve.

In Britain, these factors have perhaps contributed to the rise in the numbers of couples **cohabiting**, which is often, if not an alternative to marriage, then at least a preliminary **phase** before marriage. One effect of the trend towards 'later' commitment is that women are having children later on in life, and thus fewer of them.

5 Willmott and Young traced some of the residents relocated from Bethnal Green and concluded that a move to a working-class suburban estate represented a **loss of community**. They argued that the new accommodation facilitated the development of an entirely new style of life where relations were not 'face-to-face' but 'window-to-window'.

One way of considering changes in the experience and structure of families is in terms of **private** and **public space**. The design of the internal space of the home and the external space of the community are considered as significant influencing factors in the development of the family. The larger rooms of sixteenth and seventeenth century town houses had space for the visitor and for all the household members. However, with the advent of modernity, 'all the spaces belonging to the "communality" of the family and household have been reduced to the least possible compass' (Olsen 1986 cited in Sennett 1990). Sennett argues that there is a 'hostility' in the design of 'high-rise' accommodation, reducing the sense of living in a place of 'value'. The standardised or 'gridded' space of cities, he argues, 'subdues' those who live in the space. Sennett's advocacy of 'the humane city' can be seen in the context of British urban developments. Since the 1960s there has been a general population movement away from the centre of cities and into the suburbs. The creation of **new towns** and the work of Development Corporations altered the urban landscape over the 1970s and 1980s.

More recently schemes of urban **regeneration** have reclaimed some of the run-down areas of the city. **Gentrification** is the restoration of old buildings for new purposes, often designed specifically for those with higher incomes (e.g. Docklands). These factors combine to transform relatively small geographic areas of the city into places of great class, cultural and architectural diversity.

Now learn how to use your knowledge

Family

Use your knowledge

60 minutes

Hints

1 (a) How has the privatisation of the family reinforced the gendered organisation of housework (i.e. based on sexual difference)?

(b) How does technology affect gender relations and also how are technological developments shaped by gender? Is one more dominant than the other?

think of individual vs. collective roles

gender   techn

2 Some Marxist approaches to the family have been criticised for being 'gender-blind'. How, and to what extent, can this criticism be levelled at sociological accounts of the family?

3 A high proportion of those who divorce or separate, remarry or cohabit with a new partner. The 'reconstituted family' is a product of this trend. What are possible sociological explanations for this trend against a perceived 'failure' of previous marriage?

4 (a) Is the pessimism of Lasch's interpretation of family life founded against the backdrop of the 'reconstituted' family?
    What evidence is there to suggest that the basic family unit as a place for loving relationships and the procreation and socialisation of children will survive? What are the alternatives?

(b) In 1996, for the first time, the General Household Survey included same sex couples in their category of 'cohabiting'. Although this number was small, what implications might this have on debates about extending the definition of 'the family unit'?
    Why are 'traditional' sociological conceptualisations of the nature and structure of families in Britain largely redundant in terms of contemporary familial experience? What alternative explanations are possible?

Lasch sees the modern family as being 'under siege'

changing trends = changing theories?

5 What are the new possibilities for living in the urban spaces being created in Britain today?

diversity ≠ equality

Answers on page 66

Health

15 minutes

Test your knowledge

1 Give examples of medical and social determinants of health.

2 Factors through which social class might affect health include the lack of provision of clean _____ and good _____ , cramped _____ , as well as poor _____ , due to low income among low social class individuals.

3 Geographical region affects health. However, this seems to be a marker for _____ _____ . It may also reflect long-standing inadequacies of _____ provision in such low-income areas.

4 Gender is a major _____ determinant of health, due to the different _____ bodies and thus diseases of men and women. Gender is, however, also a major _____ determinant of health as men's and women's behaviours are constructed differently by society. A good example of this would be _____ .

5 Ethnicity and health are linked in complex ways by other social factors. These include _____ and _____ .

6 What are the two main approaches to mental health and illness?

Answers

1 social – good water and sewage provision, housing conditions, work environment; medical – vaccination programmes, availability of drugs (such as antibiotics)   2 water, sanitation, housing, diet   3 social class, medical   4 biological, physical, social, smoking   5 class, gender   6 one is medically definable, biomedical model, labels of mental illness presumed rational and scientific in basis; other is socially imposed label, largely independent of the symptoms themselves at any given time once that label has been assigned

✓ If you got them all right, skip to page 25

Health

Improve your knowledge

20 minutes

1 A classical medical approach to health sees the body as a machine. When healthy, it functions fully and properly. Illness is seen as a natural malfunction of that body, something that can be treated on an individual basis through the use of human interventions such as surgery or drugs.

By contrast, since the mid-nineteenth century in particular (the Chadwick Report) evidence appeared which contradicted this. It was shown that the provision of clean drinking water and good sewage and refuse disposal were major factors in the prevention of disease, particularly in large towns. Also adequate diet had been shown to be central to preventing diseases such as scurvy (caused by a lack of vitamin C). This showed that disease is also **socially constructed**. It was further reinforced by the work of the 1980 Black Report.

key study

There are variations in health and illness, as well as provision of health care, by class, geographical region, gender and ethnicity.

2 **Class**

The main correlation with class is **income**. Low-class households have, by definition, lower incomes than higher-class households. Thus, by definition, the *Inequalities in Health Report* (1979) identifies poverty and the relatively poor access of lower socio-economic groups to the knowledge and resources which help to maintain health (O'Donnell, 1997). Thus it can be seen that low income can force people to live in unsafe, overcrowded, polluted areas with minimal or no provision of healthy basic hygiene.

class is linked to poverty and wealth

The 1991 Nutritional Task Force, set up by the Major government, also stated that 'people on limited incomes may experience particular difficulties in obtaining a healthy and varied diet'.

3 Region

There is a clear north–south divide in **regional variation** in **mortality rates** (*Inequalities in Health Report*, 1979), with the northern areas tending to have the higher mortality rates. However, this might for example reflect the former northern industrial towns with large low social class populations compared to towns in the south. Hence the regional variations making for social class differences. Part of the regional variation might also be an associated **historical difference** in the provision of health care that has been perpetuated with time, so that the regions with the most need of health care are those with the least provision. Whilst this might be so, it is argued that **social class** and other factors are actually more important for variations in overall health in regional populations.

to what extent is the 'north-south' divide a media construction?

local politics?

4 Gender

Whilst in both men and women the primary single cause of death is **circulatory diseases** and the secondary cancers (*Social Trends*, 1992), the nature of these diseases differs by gender. For example, the major cause of cancer-related deaths in men is lung cancer (100 per 100 000 of population (*Social Trends*, 1992)). In women lung cancer (40 per 100 000) is second to breast cancer (50 per 100 000). Whilst cervical, ovarian, breast and prostate cancers can be seen, by biological necessity, to be **gender specific**, the variations in lung, stomach and colon cancers cannot. Whilst it is possible that there are gender-specific biological causes, this would suggest that these are due to **social reasons**.

Men tend to smoke more than women, which would account for men having double the rate of deaths from lung cancer than women. However, the incidence of smoking in women is **increasing**, whilst that in men is **falling**. The figures for lung cancer from 1971–1990 (*Social Trends*, 1992) reflect just this; **decreasing incidence** of male mortality from lung cancer and **increasing mortality** from lung cancer in women. (Remember though that male death rates are still roughly twice that of women for lung cancer!)

changing social roles = what pattern of health in 20 years' time?

5 Ethnicity

Ethnic groups may span a wide range of class locations. As such, the **main determinants of health** will not be ethnicity, but other factors such as class, gender and age. Thus ethnicity in itself has little effect on the social construction of health and disease.

By contrast, in accessing medical provision there may be a **social dimension**. There may be a problem due to linguistic difficulties or social and religious objections, such as a woman being afraid that the doctor that will examine her will be male. However, overall the high correlation of new immigrants with low-class living is more important here.

6 Mental health and illness

Mental health practice has been based upon a rational, scientific, **biomedical model of illness**. It relies on the use of drugs-based and other medical 'treatments'. The major problem with this system is that once labelled as 'mentally ill' that diagnosis remains with the person diagnosed. Rosenham (1978), through **social experimentation**, was able to show that diagnosis of such mental illness was prone to wide interpretation by the diagnosing doctor. As such, a high level of false positive diagnoses were observed. Thus the status of mentally ill people as 'mentally ill' can be seen to be **socially constructed**.

what is 'mentally ill'? who defines 'normal'? how? (can it be defined?)

By contrast, Michel Foucault in *Madness and Civilization* treats mental illness in a non-judgemental way. He takes a historical perspective on the way in which mental health and 'madness' has been differently constructed at different times in history.

Now learn how to use your knowledge

Health

1 Health and illness are social and not medical issues. Discuss.

2 What variations in health, if any, can be accounted for by social class? Explain with reference to specific examples.

3 What variations in health, if any, can be accounted for by regional variations? Explain with reference to specific examples.

4 What variations in health, if any, can be accounted for by gender differences? Explain with reference to specific examples.

5 What variations in health, if any, can be accounted for by ethnicity? Explain with reference to specific examples.

6 Mental illness is a medically diagnosable, permanent state of being. To what extent can this be said to be true?

Answers on page 68

Education

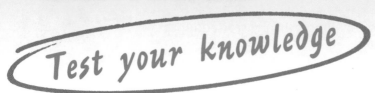

Test your knowledge

20 minutes

1 Education is seen as a primary agency of _____ and particularly in a positive way from a _____ perspective.

Durkheim proposes that education has numerous functions:

- to transmit society's _____ and _____
- to promote 'social _____'
- to teach _____ between children
- to teach the required skills for future roles and _____.

2 The perspective outlined in 1 above is broadly a functionalist approach, based on the principles of equality of opportunity in a meritocratic system of education. Identify the key principles or basis of the following perspectives on education:

(a) Marxism
(b) Feminism
(c) Interactionism.

3 The structural Marxists Bowles and Gintis (1976) argue that a major function of education is the _____ of labour power, via the _____ _____. Thus the teaching and organisation of a lesson is the focal point for the reproduction of inequality, rather than the _____ of the subject/lesson being taught.

4 Some sociological explanations of differential educational achievement take the view that the concepts 'educational success' and 'educational failure' are _____ constructed.

5 Liberal Feminists are committed to the principle of equal _____ in education and fundamental to this is equal _____. This, they believe (in contrast to other Feminist schools of thought) can be achieved through _____ reform.

Answers

curriculum', content **4** socially **5** opportunity, access, democratic
(c) classroom relationships and interaction **3** reproduction, 'hidden
ideology (b) patriarchal ideology and 'hidden curriculum'
co-operation, occupations **2** (a) reproduction of class, culture,
1 socialisation, functionalist, norms, values, solidarity,

If you got them all right, skip to page 33

26

Education

Improve your knowledge

1 Parsons' (1959) now perhaps outmoded conception of education was based on a **consensus** of normative values, attitudes and beliefs. He defined the **dual problem** of 'socialisation' and 'selection'. Whilst applying the principle of **meritocracy** in education, this simultaneously legitimates occupational and social **inequalities**. For example, as Brown et al. (1997) consider: 'the doctrine of meritocracy is based on the idea of giving everyone an equal chance to be unequal'. Brown et al. cite Young (1961) who considers that the education system faces a long-standing conflict between 'the principles of selection by **family**, and the principles of selection by **merit**'.

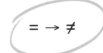

Since early sociological accounts there has been a significant shift in emphasis toward a focus on:

- culture
- knowledge
- the curriculum.

The study of differential educational attainment based on class has been joined with a growing literature examining educational inequality based on:

- gender
- race
- ethnicity.

Althusser, the French neo-Marxist, argues that the 'fit' between education and industry serves the middle-class via their organisation, language, attitudes, beliefs and culture. The lower classes are thus socialised into believing that the educational system is **fair** in terms of the differential attainment produced, so that inequalities of class are continued unchallenged. So, schools are part of the ruling-class's '**ideological state apparatus**'.

legitimising inequality

27

2 An **interactionist** perspective provides a critique of sociological accounts of differential educational attainment based on intelligence, class and deprivation. This view considers these accounts as **deterministic** – individuals are largely predisposed to act in a certain way and achieve to a certain standard. Principally, these factors can be categorised as **external** stimuli or influences.

Interactionists argue that **self**-conception of attainment or failure is produced through interaction with others. '**Others**' are the external stimuli for interactionists, with the self constantly **monitoring** (even in a kind of unconscious way) the reactions and comments of others, which **feed** in to create a continuous self-perception.

people plus environment

During the 1980s and 1990s there have been tremendous changes in the patterns of working in Britain. The notion of the **bureaucracy** as a form of mass education and the basis for mass employment is now outmoded. These changes reflect a decline in the notion of a **common culture**, the result of a system of education based on definitive mass groupings of class, culture and religion.

fragmentation

A useful definition of Bourdieu's **cultural capital** is provided by Wells (1996):

> 'a system of implicit and deeply internalised values passed down by generations and influenced by social class, ethnicity, and parents' education'.

Thus, educational qualifications are an **institutionalised** form of cultural capital.

3 Bowles and Gintis' **hidden curriculum** has four key elements.

- Production of **passive** employees to form a subservient workforce.
- Encourages acceptance of **hierarchy** and non-involvement in work, or even **alienation** from work.
- Minimal educational satisfaction leads pupils to seek **external** rewards via qualifications and potential employment.
- The **fragmentation** of the school 'working day' which is 'training' for a similar segmentation of employment later, e.g. factory assembly line.

They argue there are **structural** parallels between the economic system and education which they term the **correspondence principle**.

structural relations

Illich (1973) questions the notion of compulsory schooling, where schools have now become **custodial** organisations. The 'hidden curriculum' encourages '**passive consumption**' – an acceptance of the social hierarchy as part of the daily order of the school environment. Illich's proposed solution is through **deschooling** society and replacing the educational system with learning that is widely available, rather than within the **rigid framework** of the school environment of today. Knowledge would then become less the property of specialists and specialist environments.

Abercrombie, Ward et al. (1994) argue that schools present a **differentiated** hidden curriculum, where children are 'inexplicitly' taught **social attitudes** which prepare them to become employees.

'hidden' preparation for work

This is differentiated by:

- **gender** – male activities are typically granted higher status than females, with male behaviour traits (aggression, disorderly conduct etc.) less tolerated in girls. Gender roles and stereotypes are reinforced by teachers' differential **expectations** of potential employment prospects.
- **social class** – courses/subjects can be linked to recruitment from different class backgrounds (Banks et al., 1992).

The hidden curriculum is a 'by-product' of schooling rather than being something more tangible or visible in the way the content of subjects and courses being taught is.

However, these debates in education can be viewed as increasingly **outmoded**. New debates relate to the collapsing of the previously definitive 'fit' between education and work. These are based on the problematisation of the definition of **skill** (Block, 1990) and the change in **employer** definitions, for example, after a period defined by a kind of 'forced integration' between education and the labour market (as per Bowles and Gintis).

who defines 'skill' and how?

In the transformed **post-industrial** or **post-modern** world of work, the **criteria** for increased organisational efficiency involve **interpersonal** skills:

- communication
- negotiation
- group or 'team' work.

However, the educational establishment itself is unlikely to support wholeheartedly a fundamental move to the development of **personal** and **social skills** in education. With the increase in the numbers passing GCSE and A levels, and gaining higher qualifications, in recent years, the field of available employees has become less differentiated, when recruiting on the basis of academic qualification. The system is still geared toward the **credibility** of academia based on a degree of **objective** assessment.

more success or lower standards?

This is the position of Brown et al. who argue: 'there seems little doubt that the acquisition of **cultural capital** based on family background, education, qualification, gender, and ethnicity is increasingly having to be "**repackaged**" to incorporate those "personal qualities" that expose the subjective "inner world" of the self in the market for jobs'.

 D. H. Hargreaves (1982) argues that the curriculum and standards of the grammar school have been adopted or mimicked in the comprehensive system. This has led to the dominance of the system of public examinations and that many pupils come to experience education as failure.

The **definition** of what constitutes 'educational success' and 'educational failure' changes with time. Thus, the social construction of concepts is **temporally** relevant. For example, the **number** of persons entering higher education has increased significantly in recent years. In 1981, 5% of the population of the UK (no longer in full-time education) had a degree or equivalent qualification, whereas in 1996 this figure had more than doubled to 11%, according to the 1996 General Household Survey. So, awareness that more people were educated at this level, informed through media reporting, for example, suggests a lessening of the value

higher education

placed on the attaining of a degree. Simply, one might have a more exceptional sense of achievement or 'success' in completing a degree in 1981 than in, say, 1999.

The **'social' construction** of the concepts of 'success' and 'failure' in education, however, can be attributed to a more local influencing of self-perception. That is the way in which parents, teachers and other pupils affect and influence the progress of a pupil by virtue of their behaviour towards them. This behaviour is based on **expectation** of pupil progress.

Howard S. Becker, through interviews conducted with 60 Chicago high school teachers, found that they perceived students according to an **ideal** of work, conduct and appearance. Through this very process of perception, Becker argues that teachers subsequently experienced problems with those students they perceived as furthest away from this ideal standard.

Interactionists argue that the **typing** or **labelling** of pupils (as 'able', 'poor' or 'deviant', for example) **influences** their educational progress. For example, this can affect teachers' decisions on where to sit pupils, what courses/classes they are placed in, and what exams they are entered for.

The **predictions** made by teachers of the performance of their pupils coming true, or being 'fulfilled' is known as the theory of **self-fulfilling prophecy**. The perception of the pupil, by the teacher, based on their prediction, will affect the pupil by way of their interaction with them. Pupils' **self**-perception is influenced in this way and is likely to live up or live down to these expectations accordingly.

One way in which this process is institutionalised is through **banding** or **streaming**. That is, pupils are taught in groups according to ability or potential attainment, based on previous performance, but this can also be based on teacher perception. Overall, **labelling** is influenced by a number of factors, and can have negative as well as positive effects on pupils.

However, as Fine (1991) argues, those students from groups most likely to be labelled as 'failures' who do perform well academically 'seem to deny, repress or dismiss the stories of failure, and persist undaunted in their personal crusade against the odds' (see Wells, 1996).

Arnot and Weiner (1987) identify three Feminist perspectives that they claim have most impact upon education.

- **Liberal** Feminism – claims that as gender roles are not **innate** it should be possible to change them. Pressure can be used to create a framework in which traditional barriers which prevent women from succeeding in their chosen occupations are eventually removed.
- **Radical** Feminism – which views the exploitation of women as based on patriarchal relations. This 'second wave' of Feminism claimed that women had to become aware of the effects of male domination through a process of **women-focused education**, that of **consciousness raising**.
  Radical Feminists argue it is important to 'uncover' the processes within the 'hidden curriculum' that reproduce patriarchy. Spender (1980), found that girls' 'talk' in class (and elsewhere) is evaluated differently from boys'. Thus, talk, as a powerful tool, is 'denied' to women in patriarchal society. This is part of the (often unconscious) way in which teachers act differently towards boys and girls. The **dominance of males** and the **acquiescence of girls** is thus reinforced in the self-perception of pupils.
- **Marxist/Socialist** Feminism – this approach highlights inequality through 'class, race and gender structures and ideologies'. It examines the **interrelationship** of capitalism and patriarchy through the connection between education and the family, and the labour market.

Weiner (1994) acknowledges criticism of this classification through its marginalising of other feminisms, particularly black feminism and lesbian feminism. Black feminists argue that contemporary racism now needs to be seen as a **structural** feature of the educational and wider social system, rather than merely as a matter of individual prejudice (Brah and Minhas, 1985, cited in Weiner, 1994).

Education

Use your knowledge

1. In what ways is the education system of today a 'site of struggle' (Brown et al, 1997)? Will it always be?

   class conflict

2. With the perceived rise in affluence over the past few decades and the rise of the 'new' middle class, what implications do these socio-economic trends have when considering the relationship between class and education?

3. 'Resistance' theorists (e.g. Willis, 1977) argue that pupils from lower-class backgrounds resist the 'dominant' culture and play an active role in their own social and cultural reproduction. In what ways can this approach be used as a critique of a structuralist Marxist perspective of the education system?

   critique of passive pupils

4. How have the recent improvements in the pass marks at GCSE and A level affected the social construction of the concepts 'educational success' and 'educational failure'?

5. **Highest qualification attained by sex in the UK, 1996, according to General Household Survey, 1996.**

	Men %	Women %
Degree or equivalent	13	8
A level or equivalent	14	10
GCSE grades A–C or equivalent	21	24

   How might a broadly feminist approach explain the attainment differentiated by gender set out in the above table?

Answers on page 71

Religion

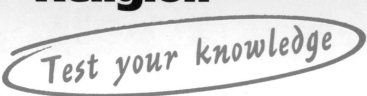

25 minutes

1 Who wrote (a) *The Protestant Ethic and the Spirit of Capitalism* (b) *Elementary Forms of the Religious Life* (c) *The German Ideology?*

2 What term is used to depict a situation in which the beliefs and sanctions of religion become increasingly discounted in society as guides to conduct or decision making?

3 (a) A _____ tends to be a large, conservative religious organisation which is supportive of the state. It is _____ as it attempts to embrace all members of society, draws its membership from all _____ _____ and children are usually _____ into it.

(b) A _____ is a small and exclusive religious group and as such requires that its members show _____ to the group and _____ in its principles. These organisations are typically _____ of the current social order and so draw their members from more marginal groups in society such as the _____, _____ _____, and the _____ _____.

(c) The increasingly sophisticated use of the media by some religious organisations as their primary means of communication with potentially simultaneously _____ congregations is known as the _____ _____. These often _____ religions based on individual purchase are characteristic of _____-_____ societies.

4 What are the three forms of New Religious Movements as characterised by Roy Wallis?

5 Which of the world's major religions are widely practised in contemporary Britain?

6 In the _____ that make up religious organisations with clear systems of authority, _____ are largely disempowered.

7 Meredith B. McGuire states that whether religion is a force for change or stasis depends on four factors. What are these four factors?

Answers **1** (a) Max Weber (b) Emile Durkheim (c) Karl Marx **2** secularisation **3** (a) church, universal, social positions/social groups/status groups, born (b) sect, commitment, faith, critical, young, ethnic minorities, working class (c) global, 'electronic church', consumerist, post-modern **4** world rejecting, world affirming, world accommodating **5** Christianity, Islam, Hinduism, Judaism, Sikhism, Buddhism **6** hierarchies, women **7** the beliefs, internal organisation and 'social location' of the religion, and the culture of the society in which a religion exists

If you got them all right, skip to page 42

34

Religion

Improve your knowledge

1   An important work in addition to the three 'classical' thinkers in the study of religion is that of **The Halevy Thesis**. Elie Halevy wanted to provide an explanation as to why despite the massive political and social instability in England in the period 1790–1830, there was no revolution. His eventual answer was that religion played the key role in pacifying any potential revolutionaries.

Halevy Thesis – Methodism prevented revolution in England

Revolutionaries could potentially come from two groups.

*   Firstly, the rising bourgeoisie who were beginning to make money and so gain great social and political influence. If they were blocked in their desires, they could be dangerous to the traditional social order as occurred in France and resulted in the French Revolution in 1789.
*   Secondly, the new urban proletariat was suffering great hardship and poverty due to the huge changes taking place because of the Agricultural and Industrial Revolutions, rapid urbanisation and the development of a capitalist money economy. Hence **pacification** was needed.

In 1739 John Wesley founded **Methodism** which provided a link between the aristocracy and the proletariat and bourgeoisie. This new denomination provided the pacification needed because:

*   Wesley was from the ruling classes and so had the **values and beliefs** of this group which he wanted to instil in the workers via preaching the word of God
*   his evangelical style was not liked by the rather staid ruling classes who constituted the Church of England. Methodists were thus cut off from the main church and became '**non-conformist**'. Methodism thus filled a social and ideological vacuum between the two groups and opened up the channels of **social** and **ideological mobility**.

Wesley began preaching to one particular group known as the Kingswood Miners, a highly motivated rebellious group, in a time of great economic and political crisis. Their revolutionary intent soon assumed a different form as their political fervour transformed into religious fervour. Although it is unclear whether the breakdown of rebelliousness occurred because of Methodism, or whether Methodism provided comfort afterwards, it is clear that the ideals and beliefs of Methodism became part of the ideas and beliefs of the revolutionary group, which must in some way have dampened their fire. Such a phenomenon is not peculiar to the Kingswood Miners but happened throughout the period of crisis, 1790–1830, and beyond.

To show how religion is the key variable which prevented a revolution in England, Halevy examines other possible variables comparing England with France.

- Both countries had **unstable political institutions** – these collapsed in France but not in England.
- Both countries suffered from **disorganised economic production** which could have made revolution possible in both places but only did so in France.

According to Halevy, the cause of the different outcomes, despite similar situations, was **religion**. In England any revolutionary zeal was drawn into religion generally, and Methodism in particular, as this provided a means for the aspiring middle classes to move up the **social ladder**. In France any aspirations were blocked by the aristocracy and without a compensatory religion to turn to, revolution occurred in France but not in England.

Thus it can be seen that Methodism provided a **stepping stone** for the potentially revolutionary middle class who were gaining a good deal of power in society. This stepping stone, though, not only enabled social mobility, it also passed the **ideology of the ruling class** down to the lower orders.

2 The cult of individualism

As Durkheim argued, the collective conscience of society is integrated through **religious rituals**, prayers, ceremonies, saying grace. In the modern world, however, such religious beliefs and rituals, which represent the whole of society, seem so general and remote as to disappear from everyday life. Erving Goffman, a follower of Durkheim, argued that although such rituals have gone, others – called **interaction rituals** – have emerged in their place. These rituals take place in our everyday conversations and are often what we ordinarily think of as **politeness**. The sacred object or ideal attached to them is no longer society as a whole, but rather the individual self.

see Durkheim on the relationship between individualism and society

In contrast to traditional tribal societies where individuals conceive themselves as **part of the clan**, in modern societies each individual is held to have an inner-self, a **subjectivity**. However, according to Randall Collins, this subjectivity does not simply exist in our 'selves', in our individual psychological make-up, it is constructed through our interaction rituals. This can be seen in everyday conversations where we constantly tell 'white lies' to exaggerate and build up incidents in our lives, to make ourselves look smarter, cooler or more successful than we actually are. We allow others to do the same so that we mutually build up ourselves and one another.

The modern self is like any other sacred object created by **social rituals** – it is largely a **myth**. We are nowhere near as autonomous or individualistic as we tell ourselves and others we are. Behind the modern subjective self, then, is **society**. It is a way that we, as a group, can maintain **integration and cohesion** in a world with a highly complex division of labour.

3 Post-modernity and religion I

Where traditional societies were integrated by religion, and modern societies experienced secularisation (as the 'grand narratives' of freedom and equality, of Marxism and the rational scientific order came to replace unscientific, irrational beliefs in the supernatural) post-modernists claim contemporary society no longer believes in such 'grand narratives'. We now recognise that there can be no ultimate, rational way of organising the world for the benefit of all, that it is unrealistic to think that there are long-term directional trends and that we are moving towards a better, or worse, society for all. Rather, post-modernists would point to the rise of 'consumerist' religions where we can 'buy into', often literally, religious or spiritual experiences and beliefs which:

- support our own world view
- support our own lifestyle
- enable us to be or to 'find' ourselves.

lifestyles and consumerism

'grand narratives' = overarching idea on how society should be organised for the benefit of all, e.g. liberalism, rationalism, Marxism

4 Post-modernity and religion II

A new religious movement might also be considered to be a feature of post-modernism. However, some might argue that post-modernity is not a **global phenomenon** but then neither was modernity. The project of modernity merely reflected the self-assurance of the West in its own 'grand schemes' for imposing its own order upon the world. Post-modernism, too, is a Western theory which reflects the **relativisation of the West** due to globalisation. A West which is no longer in control of itself, let alone the rest of the world, has responded by claiming that the modern project is dead and so denying 'grand narratives'. However, grand narratives are not dying in Latin America or Asia, indeed their religious vitality (consider the rise of Islamic fundamentalism and the Islamic Revolution in Iran) is in part a response to the precarious state of the grand narrative in the West. Religion is therefore far from dead, for it is playing a crucial role in the 'new world order' – although less so within most of Europe (Robertson).

globalisation

5 Multiculturalism

Religious pluralism is not new, nor is it unusual. Indeed, in our increasingly connected and mobile world it is now probably the norm rather than the exception. However, the nature of religious pluralism will depend upon the specific situation and circumstances and will vary from country to country, and from religion to religion. Therefore, as broad generalisations are unlikely to be helpful we will instead give a brief overview of the main non-Christian religions.

multiculturalism in Britain

The **British Jewish community** numbers around 330 000 and is concentrated in particular areas: notably London, Manchester, Leeds and Glasgow. The population has declined this last half century, from a peak of about 400 000 in the 1950s, due to migration to Israel, marriage outside the community and decreasing family size. However, it is the fifth largest Jewish community in the world after the US, Israel, the former Soviet Union and France.

The **Muslim community** is difficult to number and is one of the most diverse religious communities given the varied backgrounds of this group. It is estimated that there are just over one million of the Islamic faith in Britain, although the actively religious population is rather less. The majority of Muslims originate from Pakistan and Bangladesh. The former tend to live in Bradford and the West Midlands, the latter in London's East End.

The issue of religious pluralism in general and Muslims in Britain in particular came to a head several years ago with 'The Rushdie Affair'. Questions were raised about how a secular society can accommodate a strongly religious group. Must it destroy religiosity and difference so that everyone can be equal or can it encourage tolerance and diversity even if this undermines the project of modernity, and its grand narratives of freedom and equality?

Finally, the **sociology of religion** links to the **sociology of locality** and **community** again, but this time in recognising that, although we do live in a multicultural society, some areas are more culturally diverse than others. Hence the politics of religion and race are linked to social geography and to local culture and economics.

Gender and religion

One way of looking at the internal organisation of religion is through a focus on gender. Both quantitatively and qualitatively women's experiences of religion are different to those of men.

Quantitatively, women are much more likely to go to church than men. The evidence for this is overwhelming and has been for many years. However, despite this there has been little research in this area since traditional sociology of religion has been less concerned with gender, and Christian feminists have been more concerned with the power of men in the chancel. Thus, there is no convincing explanation.

Statistics on churchgoing:
(Percentage of female churchgoers)

England	(1979)	55%
England	(1989)	58%
Wales	(1982)	62%
Scotland	(1984)	66%

(Source: G. Davie, 1995)

what issues do the use of these statistics raise?

One possible explanation involves age and generation. The ratio of females to males increases with every step up the age scale, therefore there are disproportionate numbers of women in congregations, especially in the more elderly congregations. However, although this may account for some of the difference it cannot account for it all.

Moreover, there is a difference in men's and women's conceptions of religion and God. Women concentrate more on the God of love, comfort and forgiveness than on the God of power, planning and control which, when asked to describe the God in whom they believe, is the God men emphasise.

Grace Davie, in trying to understand both these quantitative and qualitative differences argues that the most likely explanation is the proximity of women to birth and death. Very few women, according to Davie, give birth without any thought about existence and creation. Similarly, watching someone die, especially someone close encourages thoughts about the meaning of their life and what might happen to them after death. Given then that women remain primarily responsible for the care of the elderly and dying as well as the nurture of the young, it is hardly surprising they are more religious as measured by church attendance and have the conception of God they do. However, Davie reminds us that the evidence remains impressionistic and far from proven.

Davie links qualitative + quantitative evidence

7 **Puritanism, individualism and housing style**
We can trace contemporary religion in Britain partly through historical development, e.g. in relation to Puritanism. Following Weber in exploring the impact of Protestantism on the modern world, Matthew Johnson argues that Puritanism was one of a number of important factors in West Sussex which led to changes in the structure of the 'typical' house. He explores how house styles changed in this part of England between the fifteenth and seventeenth centuries, reflecting a wider change in social relations.

avoids problem of reductionism (there are other causal factors)

Thus in the early part of this period, the late medieval times, houses were marked by a series of features which indicated an 'open' society, whereby status was recognised and social relations were conducted at the face-to-face level, reflecting typically 'gemeinschaft relations'. Such features included a large central hall which went straight up to the rafters, thus through height denoting status, and in which much local public activity took place. Within the hall was an open fire and a front door which led directly from outside the house into the hall, illustrating the public-centredness of the space. There was little functional distinction between rooms as people ate and slept in all rooms, including the hall. Upstairs rooms were mainly for storage, rather than for privacy.

'gemeinschaft' = a social grouping held together by friendship or kinship ties

By contrast the closed house was one which reflected the capitalist, class-based society and the increasingly private nature of social relations, families etc. The door opened onto a lobby rather than into the hall, the fire was shifted to a chimney stack, the hall had a mezzanine floor put in so that the upper floor could be used fully without coming downstairs. Rooms began to take on more specific and particular functions, beds were no longer placed anywhere, the skin of the house was covered over and decoration and display moved inside particularly in terms of moveable goods, pewter tankards, plates etc.

For our argument here though, Johnson links these overall changing social relations as reflected in changing house and agricultural forms to changing religion, and especially the growth of Puritanism in the area. With its emphasis on privacy, individuality and fear of neighbours (need to keep doors locked at night to keep evil spirits away), the closed house reflected well the **changing social relations**. For Johnson, it is a mistake to see changing house form as simply a more rational way of doing things, or a development in building techniques. For the craft techniques previously employed were intimately tied to the way of life, to the culture of the area and period. Only when this culture started to change could the economically rational and the functional ideas of capitalism about room use, building techniques etc. fully come into play.

Now learn how to use your knowledge

Religion

Use your knowledge

75 minutes

Hints

1 'Religion can never die – it merely changes to meet the needs of society.' What might be the key points of such an argument? What do you think are the strengths and weaknesses of such an argument?

2 Many theories of religion use typologies to define what a church, denomination, sect or cult is. Why might sociologists want to use such typologies? What is the problem with these typologies?

think phenomenologically

3 Outline the arguments for and against the secularisation thesis.

4 It can be argued that the functionalist or anthropological approach as exemplified by Durkheim and Malinowski is only really applicable to small-scale, 'traditional' societies. Why might this be the case?

5 If secularisation is an aspect of modernity, what impact might post-modernism have on the relationship between religion and society?

6 How might sport be understood as a religion?

Durkheim – cult of individualism

7 What is 'ideology'? What is the relationship between religion and ideology according to the Marxists? Why does religion justify the interests of the bourgeoisie?

Answers on page 72

Power and politics

15 minutes

1 Power is an 'essentially contested concept' (Lukes 1974). What are the three broad models of the distribution of power in Britain?

(a) _____ _____ (power based on ownership – bourgeoisie versus proletariat).

(b) _____ (power concentrated via organised groups and interests and through systematic political bias).

(c) _____ (fragmented and dispersed power influenced by competing groups).

2 According to Weber, _____ power is exercised through authority (power that is acknowledged as being justly exercised). He identified three broad forms of authority:

(a) _____ (established patterns of behaviour)

(b) _____ (personality of leaders)

(c) _____ (structured in rules/law).

3 The modern state consists of a diverse set of social institutions that are at the centre of a geographically bounded _____ which is managed by the political apparatus of government through the ultimate threat of _____ force. Modern _____-states operate under rule of _____ which is the right of supreme authority in a clearly defined area.

4 Goldthorpe and Lockwood looked for evidence of change in the political affiliation and traditional values of workers following increased prosperity in Luton in their study of *The Affluent Worker* (1963). They claimed that despite evidence of the workforce becoming instrumental and privatised, this did not lead to confirmation of the _____ thesis (that increased affluence led to a change in class and political affiliation). (Labour duly won the 1964 and 1966 elections.)

5 The mass media has a long-term effect on the political process by _____ a system of parliamentary democracy.

Answers

1 (a) ruling-class (b) élite (c) pluralist   2 legitimate (a) traditional (b) charismatic (c) legal–rational   3 territory, legitimate, nation, sovereignty   4 embourgeoisement   5 perpetuating

✓ *If you got them all right, skip to page 50*

43

Power and politics

Improve your knowledge

30 minutes

1 (a) **The ruling-class approach**

Maintains that class is an example of **structured social inequality** found in all advanced societies. The state is largely the **instrument** of the capitalist owning class.

Marxist theory is tied to a model of the workings of **capitalism**, that the basis of power is found in the relations to the means of production. However Weber (1864–1920) presents a set of concepts: **social class**, **status** and **power**. He provided a more pluralistic model of different classes:

rigid structural approach

more diffuse structure

- working class (unskilled)
- the 'petty bourgeoisie'
- technicians, officials, bureaucrats
- property-owning class.

Also, Weber did not conclude (as Marx did) that classes would necessarily develop **class consciousness**. Instead, Weber uses the notion of **status** as a basis of stratification. He examined the most common organisational structure – the **bureaucracy** – and claimed that its key features were:

Weber + bureaucracy

- a hierarchy of authority
- a specialised division of tasks
- a formal set of rules acting to co-ordinate operations
- a body of workers carrying out those tasks in accordance with the hierarchy.

These are the characteristics of Weber's **ideal type** bureaucracy where **authority** can be represented in the form of a pyramid shape.

(b) **Élite theory**

The central institutions (in government, education, business, finance, judiciary, media etc.) in Britain are made up of élites who recruit from their own ranks. A striking example is PM John Major's first Cabinet (November 1990). It contained no women, 17 of its 21 members had been to Oxford or Cambridge (Oxbridge), and 19 had been to Independent schools. The position of an élite is reinforced through ensuring that decisions are made in their own interests and with links to other élites. They also manipulate the political **agenda**.

unequal access to power

self-perpetuating élites

Classical élite theorists: Mosca, Pareto and Michels.

An **oligarchy** is the **undemocratic** rule by a small group, an élite or leadership. Michels (1911), writing on 'Political Parties', suggested an 'iron law of oligarchy', namely that 'who says organisation says oligarchy'. That is, in any political system or party, there will inevitably be a minority who rule and a majority that are ruled. Pareto argued that there is a **circulation** of élites and emphasised their psychological composition ('lions' and 'foxes'). Mosca used the term 'political class' and focused on the effect of social forces. He argued that the rule by an élite is based on **organisation**, a small group being easier to organise than a large one.

Margaret Thatcher? Tony Blair?

(c) **Liberal/pluralist or representative élite theory**

Dahl in *Who Governs?* (1961) critiques the ruling élite model in a study in the US and argues power is not concentrated but revolves around decision-making processes and **issue areas**. Often there is a plurality of groups involved in each issue that compete to influence government policy. This approach is also known as a **democratic** élite perspective because of its emphasis on the role of elections to keep the political élite 'in check'.

the case for democracy

C. Wright-Mills, in his study of *The Power Elite* (1956) in the US, argued that power is concentrated in the **institutions** of the **economy**, **politics** and the **military**, who ran the country for their own benefit and against 'the masses' below them. He criticises those who use the term 'ruling class' as a 'badly-loaded phrase' given that it does not consider the possibility of autonomy in the political order, nor include the military.

inadequacy of 'class'-based accounts?

2 In the British state, power and authority pertain to a recognisable sphere in which the institutions of government operate. Government has a very broad range of powers.

- The virtually unlimited ability to make and enforce **laws**. The September 1998 recall of both the Irish and British Parliaments from their summer recess to implement new security measures is an example of the supreme power of the state to legislate at speed when it deems it to be necessary.
- The ability to raise huge sums of money through taxation.
- The employment of large numbers of people, especially in national institutions/services (e.g. the NHS). During the 1980s and 1990s, however, privatisation significantly reduced the number of direct employees of the government.
- The control of land (through ownership and regulation).
- The control of the means of economic policy through influencing exchange and interest rates and the money supply.

(See Abercrombie, Warde et al. (1994) for a clear and comprehensive perspective on the power and organisation of the British state.)

state

power

government

3 Miliband (1969) argues that Marxist theory can be applied to modern capitalist states via the **state system**. He argues there is a capitalist class who make up a '**state élite**' and who share a common social background. They seek to defend capitalist interests through the state and **legitimise** their power through their control of the **agencies of socialisation**.

A critical perspective of Miliband is offered by the Marxist structuralist Poulantzas, who argues that the state is **relatively autonomous** from the ruling class, but that it is a **cohesive** factor in securing the long-term interests of capitalism. Poulantzas divides the 'apparatuses' or 'institutions' of the state system into those which have a 'principally repressive role' (e.g. central government institutions) and others which have a 'principally ideological role' (e.g. education, family and the mass media). It is this latter group, the 'ideological state apparatus' (Althusser) that is responsible for bringing about working-class conformity.

repression and ideology

Gramsci, through his concept of **hegemony**, argued that control and consent is achieved through a varying combination of repression and ideology, in different societies at different times.

The **dominant ideology thesis** is based on a particular interpretation of Marx – that most class societies' **beliefs** and **values** are those which serve the interests of the dominant class. Subordinate classes and groups are 'misled' and uncritically accept the existing rule of law and social order. They may develop a 'false consciousness' and break away from working-class cultural values.

The dominant ideology thesis is critiqued by Abercrombie et al. (1980) who argue that the importance of ideology is greatly exaggerated by Marxists and sociologists. They suggest a solution in considering ideologies as '**sets of practices**, or as "real" **social relations**'. These, they claim, are necessary for class societies to function, although they act to conceal the nature of these societies from their members. The notions of ownership and control are separated in **managerial** theories of power, where a new managerial class come to dominate. They do not own the means of production, but they **control** it. (Burnham, *The Managerial Revolution*, 1941.)

whose ideology?

are managers a cohesive 'class'?

4 Butler and Stokes (1969) claimed that the influence of social class led to voters developing long-term identification to a particular political party. They found that most British voters possessed a **partisan self-image** – a psychological commitment to a party. The strongest single influence in this respect is **parental partisanship**.

Since the early 1970s however, **partisan dealignment** (the decline of voters identifying with one particular party) and **class dealignment** (the decline of one particular class identifying with one party) have become popular components of explanations for changes in voting behaviour in Britain.

voting behaviour research/study = 'psephology'

In an ICM poll for *The Guardian* (13 March 1992) just prior to the 1992 General Election, in answer to the question 'What is stronger, your liking for the party you support, or your dislike of the others?', 22% claimed a stronger liking of their own party, whilst 48% claimed to dislike others more. This is perhaps evidence of a weakening of party alignment.

negative images

With the election of four successive Conservative governments (1979, 1983, 1987 and 1992) shifts in the nature of the working class were identified as one possible explanation of voting behaviour. Crewe (1987) argued that following the 1983 and 1987 elections 'The Labour vote remained largely working class, but the working class was no longer largely Labour'. He describes a 'skilled, secure and affluent new working class', characterised by owner-occupation, non-unionised and private sector jobs and concentration of support in the south of the country. In 1987 it was amongst this group that a further swing to the Conservatives had occurred. Meanwhile, Labour had come to represent a 'declining segment of the working class – the traditional working class of the council estates, the public sector, industrial Scotland and the North'. It had become a 'regional class party'.

According to Crewe, in 1987, 'Had electors voted solely on the main **issues** Labour would have won'. Perhaps it was a question of voters believing the transformation of Labour. Even before their 1992 defeat, for example, Labour were accused of jettisoning their long-standing principles in an attempt to gain electoral credibility, as Hughes and Wintour (1990) argue: 'Labour's values and the people's values were – abracadabra – identical'.

a price 'well worth paying'?

 Recently the power of the mass media to affect the political process has been realised to an even greater extent. This has led to a greater sensitivity on the part of political parties in respect of their perception of their representation, particularly when in government they are responsible for the **regulation** of those media organisations.

The **style** of campaigning has been transformed with parties employing **media managers** or '**spin doctors**' to ensure that the **issues** on which they have most support receive maximum media exposure. Also, particularly when events don't go a party's way, the best possible **spin** or version of events is presented. **Pseudo-events** are those created to maximise media exposure. But there is the danger of miscalculation; for example, Labour's 1987 Sheffield Rally was viewed as 'triumphalistic' and 'machoistic' amongst a majority of C2 women voters.

The perception of the Conservative Party as 'divided' is widely held as a contributory factor to the election of the new Labour government in May 1997. In August 1998, Labour appointed Dr Jack Cunningham as the so-called 'Cabinet Enforcer', responsible for the government 'singing from the same hymn sheet'. Part of this move follows the electronic media's instant access to archives, where contradictory statements and broken pledges by politicians can be replayed **televisually**.

unity = popularity?

The political power of television (over radio) was first significantly demonstrated in the 1960 US televised debate between Presidential candidates Richard Nixon and John F. Kennedy. Radio listeners believed that Nixon had won the debate, whereas TV viewers believed that Kennedy had. Politicians are now 'groomed' to look good televisually. For instance, Michael Foot, Labour's leader in 1983 was much maligned for wearing a duffle coat to the Remembrance Day parade at the Cenotaph; Labour were so impressed with the effect of the 1987 TV party election broadcast, since dubbed 'Kinnock, The Movie', they gave it a repeat showing. By 1997, such was the sensitivity of the political parties as to the potential positive or negative effects of a TV 'head-to-head' between party leaders, that no agreement was reached, and there were threats of legal action from the smaller parties, should they be excluded.

At Prime Minister's Question Time (now televised live) both John Major and William Hague, when facing Tony Blair, attempted to ridicule him by identifying the 'sound-bite' in his speech. Namely, the sentence or phrase deliberately crafted so that it is more likely to be 'picked up' by the television evening news and other media.

talking through, or for, the medium?

In the media-saturated environment of late modernity, public opinion through polls, focus groups etc., is quickly 'fed back' into the party machinery attempting to make itself electable.

Power and politics

Use your knowledge

50 minutes

Hints

1 Compare and contrast Marxist and Weberian approaches to the exercise and legitimation of power in Britain. Why might Weber's approach to power be more useful to sociologists over time?

2 Which theory most adequately explains the distribution of power in Britain today?

3 Has there been a 'managerial revolution' as Burnham predicted?

who runs modern industries?

4 For the first General Election ever, Labour actually outscored the Conservatives among the middle class and among home-owners (41 to 35%) (Butler and Kavanagh, 1997). 'On the long road to its 1997 election victory the Labour Party has had to reinvent itself and now no longer represents the interests of the working class.'

dissolving of 'traditional' class distinctions

To what extent do you agree or disagree with this statement, and why?

5 The 1997 Labour General Election victory was marked by a turnaround in the attention given to different issues by the media. On TV and radio (BBC1, ITV, Channel 4 and Radio 4), for example, the three most covered issues were (1) Europe, (2) The Constitution and (3) Sleaze. Out of these, only 'The Constitution' had appeared in the Top 10 of 1992 (Harrison, 1997).

In the press, the issues that received the most front-page lead stories were (1) European Union, (2) Party strategies/prospects and (3) Tatton/sleaze, with only Party strategies/prospects appearing on a significant number of front pages in the run-up to the 1992 election (Scammell and Harrop, 1997).

Given the greater media attention paid to some issues at the expense of others, particularly during election campaigns, what part does the media play in the political process?

who sets the political agenda?

Answers on page 74

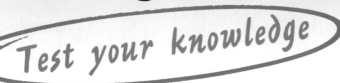

Theory and methods

30 minutes

1 Briefly define and differentiate between:

(a) structural theories   (b) social action theories.

Classify the following into the two approaches above: Marxism, Symbolic Interactionism, Ethnomethodology, Functionalism, Weberianism, Phenomenology.

2 Structural perspectives can be divided into:

(a) a _____ approach as embodied in the work of Durkheim, Parsons and Merton

(b) a _____ approach as embodied in the work of Karl Marx.

3 Crucial to the work of Durkheim, Parsons and Merton is the notion that society can be studied as a _____. This assumption enables analysis of relational phenomena as 'total social facts', through objective, observational and thus _____ research methods.

4 _____ claimed 'Action is only done by individuals' and the assumptions of the natural sciences are not adequate for the study of people. People have 'consciousness' and 'meanings', and thus it is necessary to _____ the logics that direct the actions of 'actors'.

5 Social action theorists tend to employ _____ research methods based upon in-depth analysis of a specific instance of a phenomenon. Structural researchers are more likely to utilise large-scale _____ data, i.e. many phenomena of a given 'type'.

6 Differentiate between 'primary' and 'secondary' data.

Answers

1 (a) structuralist approach emphasises the importance of social structures and minimises the importance of individual action (b) social action approaches do the reverse. Marxism and Functionalism are structuralist, Weberianism, Phenomenology, Symbolic Interactionism and Ethnomethodology are primarily social action oriented   **2** (a) conflict (b) consensus   **3** system, scientific (or positivistic)   **4** Weber, interpret   **5** qualitative, quantitative   **6** 'primary data' are collected by researcher for his or her own work, 'secondary data' already exist

If you got them all right, skip to page 60

Theory and methods

Improve your knowledge

45 minutes

1   Sociology is not unified in terms of theory or method, and is not a completed project. There are a large number of different perspectives involved which can be very roughly represented as a family tree.

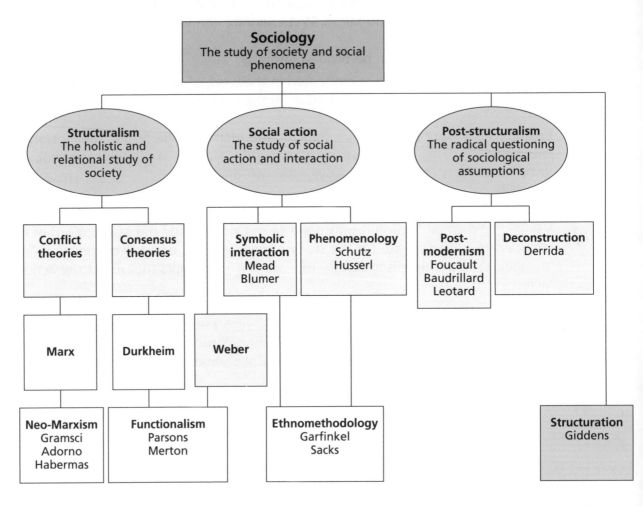

Notwithstanding the recent post-structuralist movement, sociological theories have been traditionally divided into 'Structuralist' and 'Social Action' perspectives.

Structuralism

- Denotes those perspectives which analyse 'societies' in terms of the way that components fit together, i.e. from a **'macro'** angle. Both Marx and Durkheim characterised society in terms of a 'model'. The functionalists, Parsons and Merton for example (one of which Durkheim is often considered to be) did likewise. These perspectives largely portray human action as being determined by society.

determinism

Social action approaches

- Portray human action as determining the meanings and nature of society. They view societies from a **'micro'** angle. Max Weber initially proposed this perspective, arguing that people's actions must be observed and interpreted so that their meanings can be appreciated before any attempt at explanation can be made. This notion is further developed in symbolic interactionism.

action interpretation meanings

Symbolic interactionism

- Founded chiefly by George Herbert Mead, where social structure is regarded as a fluid entity constantly changing in response to interactive concerns.

Ethnomethodology

- Draws on both symbolic interactionism and the philosophical themes of **phenomenology**, where social reality is considered to be no more than the sum of the definitions and categorisations used by members of society. Harold Garfinkel, the founder of **ethnomethodology**, denies the existence of determinate structure outright, arguing that the only force it has exists in the meanings people create for it. Furthermore, Garfinkel argues that structural theories portray people as 'Cultural Dopes', unable to reason about their actions and slavishly following cultural and social codes.

'ethnomethodology' – uses a combination of different methods

This distinction does not hold absolutely as:

- Weber, for example, maintained a concept of 'social structure'
- there is an action dimension in Marx's analysis of society
- Talcott Parsons' functionalist 'General Theory of Action' draws explicitly on an interpretation of Weber's action-oriented work.

Furthermore, Anthony Giddens' theory of **'Structuration'** makes an attempt at uniting the considerations of both structural and action theories and is not easily categorised at all.

2 Structural theories themselves can be broadly divided into a 'consensus' (Durkheim, Parsons, Merton) group and a 'conflict' group (largely, though not exclusively, Marxist thought). The key difference is in the way that the overarching 'structure' is characterised.

Consensus Theories, often functionalism – seek to analyse the way in which the 'system' operates in a harmonious and efficient way. Durkheim, for example, drawing on the works of Auguste Comte and Herbert Spencer, argued that the various parts of society were held together by a **shared consciousness** which has a religious or moral character. Social action is, then, for Durkheim, explained by the contribution it makes to this **conscience collective**. Parsons stressed that if society is to operate properly as a system, it requires the functional contributions of certain types of structure. Structural changes are determined by a culture, that is a set of values (or a **normative system)**, common to all the members of a society.

cultural values

Conflict Theories, or critical structuralism – address the imbalances in the system. This is most commonly associated with Karl Marx and Friedrich Engels, who suggested that there was always potential for conflict in the social system due to the ill-fitting nature of the parts, particularly the divisions into **social classes**. Rather than as a closely functioning set of parts, Marx characterises a 'society' as resting upon an **infrastructure** (an economic base) with a **superstructure** rising above it. Neo-Marxists have assimilated other theorists into their critical structuralism to transcend the **economic determinism** of which Marx himself is often accused. Antonio Gramsci with his concept of 'Hegemony', and The Frankfurt School (most famously Theodor Adorno) with their 'Critical Theory', add in Weberian concerns to their analyses to show how ruling-class ideologies can come to dominate the consciousness, and Jürgen Habermas links his project to **symbolic interactionism**, **functionalism** and **phenomenology** to show how meanings themselves can be 'corrupted' by powerful **bureaucracies**.

class

ideology

3 For Durkheim, like Comte, sociology was to be seen as a 'scientific' or 'positivistic' enterprise. It should be 'value free' – that is, the sociologist should abstain from making judgements about what is good or bad in society. In the famous *Rules of Sociological Method* he stipulated that the methods of the natural sciences, that is the empirical observation, categorisation and analysis of phenomena, could be applied to the study of societies. The major features of a **social system**, for Durkheim, its inherent belief systems, customs and institutions could be treated as objectively measurable things. These things are '**social facts**', which are external to, and come to determine the beliefs and actions of, any given

'value free' sociology

individual. His positivistic method can be seen at work in the famous *Suicide: A Study in Sociology*, in which he took the suicide rates of different societies as characteristic 'social facts' from which to build theory.

suicide

This was a four-stage process.

- **Observation of social fact** – in this case, the incidences of suicide in a society.
- **Statistical classification** – because social facts have an objective existence, it is possible to classify them as sets and analyse them as statistical data. Thus suicide rates in different societies could be compared.

= positivism

- **Correlation of data with other social facts** – in this Durkheim discovered a correlation between high suicide rates and Protestantism and between low suicide rates and Catholicism. He also found that high suicide rates closely correlated with high levels of education.
- **Explanation and theory generation** – Durkheim then looked for reasons for such correlations. He concluded that suicide rates depended upon levels of social integration and regulation, and isolated four different types of suicide:
    - egoistic (the result of insufficient integration, as in predominantly Protestant societies)
    - altruistic (the result of sacrifice, which would only happen in very well-integrated groups)
    - fatalistic (the result of over-regulation of the individual by society, oppression)
    - anomic (the result of under-regulation of the individual by society, causing a crisis of meaning).

This mode of analysis appears in similar forms in much of the work of Parsons and especially of Merton, whose reliance on **quantitative** statistical data is substantial. It is important to remember, also, that Durkheim considered sociology to be a 'science' according to a very specific and unified definition of what a 'science' is, a definition which has been extensively questioned in twentieth century sociology by the likes of Thomas Kuhn.

what is 'science'?

4 Contrary to Durkheim, Marx and Parsons, Max Weber explicitly rejected the **reification** of structure, the granting of objective status to it, in social study in favour of networks of social relations. He argues: ' . . . for instance, one of the most important aspects of a modern state, precisely as a complex of social interaction of individual persons, consists in the fact that the action of various individuals is oriented to the belief that it exists or should exist, thus that its acts and laws are valid in the legal sense . . . '.

Structure, then, only has meaning when people believe in it and orient their actions accordingly. Sociology, thus, as a discipline concerned with the **interpretative understanding** of social action, had to begin with empirical analysis of the social actions concerned via:

- *Verstehen*
- the direct observational (*aktuelles Verstehen*)
- explanatory, motivational (*erklärendes Verstehen*) understanding of actions and their meanings. This is done by firstly watching actions, and then attempting to place oneself in the position of the actor. Only, for Weber, after such rigorous analysis has been conducted can any causal explanations or definitions possibly be posited. His methodology is primarily a **qualitative** one. While Weber did not believe that sociological investigation could be 'value free' in the same way that Durkheim did, he only believed that values invariably affected sociologists in terms of their choice of topic; research into the topic itself could be objective. He was clear, however, like Durkheim, that sociologists should not make 'value judgements' in their work.

5

Qualitative, adj. concerned with or depending upon quality.
Quantitative, adj. 1(a) concerned with quantity, (b) measured or
measurable by quantity.

*two types of
data*

(Source: *The Concise Oxford Dictionary*)

As established, Durkheim uses chiefly **quantitative** data in his research,
whereas Weber's approach has a more **qualitative** focus. While
quantitative data take numerical form, such as the official statistics with
which Durkheim worked, the qualitative data used particularly by
interpretative sociologists interested in social action (which, of course, has
to be interpreted) take a large number of forms.

The **symbolic interactionists**, primarily interested how action is governed
by the way that people interpret the world, seldom consider quantitative
data to be a useful resource. Herbert Blumer, like Erving Goffman, rejects
Durkheim's **positivistic methodology** as crude and simplistic, arguing that
it takes no account of the views of people ('social actors') themselves and
instead imposes the researcher's own categories upon their lives. As such,
scientific methods in the study of society do much to distort social reality
and little to capture it. Rather than attempt to study social life from the
'outside', fitting data into presupposed categories, then, Blumer proposes
it be studied from the 'inside'. One of the main qualitative methods used
in order to try to understand social actors' own view of reality is
participant observation. This method is operationalised in Howard S.
Becker's study *Outsiders* in which Becker joined a group of marijuana
users for some time, observing and recording their entire way of life. The
ethnomethodologists pursue similar research methods, taking them
further still in arguing that the only way to genuinely understand and
describe the meanings and methods in the life of, say, a scientist is to live
the life of a scientist for the duration of the research. The qualitative data
that such strategies produce usually take the form of rich and detailed
field reports.

'outsiders'

description

6 As mentioned in *Test your knowledge*:

- **primary sources** are those data gathered by a researcher during the course of his or her own work
- **secondary sources** are those data which have been collected by somebody else for the purposes of a different project, including the interpretations and conclusions of the project itself.

Commonly used techniques in primary research include:

- participant observation
- 'closed' questionnaires, giving a respondent a limited choice of answers to a question, or space only to provide a short answer to a highly specific question
- 'open' questionnaires, allowing respondents to provide longer answers to more general questions
- tightly scheduled interviews, effectively 'verbal questionnaires'
- unstructured interviews, the interviewer having no predetermined questions and the interview taking the form of an open conversation.

These primary techniques can yield quantitative or qualitative data. While participant observation will yield almost exclusively qualitative data and 'closed' questionnaires will produce highly quantified results, 'open' questionnaires encourage larger sequences of text which can be treated as qualitative data in itself or interpreted and coded as quantitative data according to pre-set categories.

Commonly used secondary sources include:

- official statistics
- government reports
- journal articles
- diaries
- news reports.

Again, these sources can take quantitative or qualitative form, and furthermore can be analysed using quantitative or qualitative methods. While official statistics are clearly quantitative and lend themselves to quantitative research, government reports, like 'open' interview data, can be taken as interpretations of phenomena or coded as data themselves. News reports have become more a topic of analysis in themselves than a source of information, with textual methods such as '**discourse analysis**' being applied to undermine their claims to 'facticity' and to expose their contingencies and constructed natures.

all of these are 'texts' in themselves available for analysis

There are strengths and weaknesses in the use of all the techniques and sources listed above. These will be further elaborated in the *Use your knowledge* section. It is valuable to note, however, that few researchers today limit themselves to using only primary or secondary sources, quantitative or qualitative data. Combinations of all of the above are frequently employed in social research. This is known as '**Methodological Pluralism**'; using one 'type' of technique to verify another is known as '**Triangulation**'.

Theory and methods

Use your knowledge

90 minutes

Hints

1. Outline the main criticisms of quantitative research made by interpretative sociologists.

2. What is *Verstehen*? What is its influence upon Symbolic Interactionism and Ethnomethodology?

3. In *Anti-Minotaur: The Myth of a Value-Free Sociology*, Alvin Gouldner argues that 'If sociologists ought not to express their personal values, how then are students to be safeguarded against the unwitting influence of these values which shape the sociologist's selection of problems, his preferences for certain hypotheses or conceptual schemes and his neglect of others? For these are unavoidable and, in this sense, there can be no value-free sociology. The only choice is between an expression of one's values, as open and honest as one can be . . . and a vain ritual of moral neutrality which, because it invites men to ignore the vulnerability of reason to bias, leaves it at the mercy of irrationality.' Against whom is he arguing? What is the problem with his argument?

4. What do Functionalism and Marxism have in common? How do they differ?

   'types' of theory

5. 'The rather partisan either/or tenor of debate about quantitative and qualitative research may appear somewhat bizarre for an outsider, for whom the obvious way forward is likely to be a fusion of the two approaches so that their respective strengths might be reaped.' (Alan Bryman, *Quantity and Quality in Social Research*). What is he talking about? Which methods have been tied to which theories? What is 'Triangulation'? What are its strengths?

   qualitative vs. quantitative?

6. Differentiate between Sociology and Social Policy.

Answers on page 76

Answers to

Use your knowledge tests

Mass media

1 Advertising phrases and products are tailored for different media. However, certain images/names/stars become iconic – they come to symbolise a product that is immediately recognisable within any culture that has been exposed to global branding.

In some advertising, the product itself no longer has to appear in order for the product or brand to be recognised.

2 Whereas 'old' media consisted of the means of communications themselves, 'new' media is about the control and flow of information. This is a useful distinction in the argument that the very nature of the media is changing – particularly with the advent of the World Wide Web that raises issues about ownership and power based on access to information.

A post-modern perspective on the move to a media-saturated environment, might consider that an overload of messages and signs causes disorientation and fragmentation of culture and identity. We are literally overwhelmed by media messages in the post-modern environment, to the extent that we lose a sense of 'meaning'.

3 The introduction of Western consumerist culture via advertising into underdeveloped countries may lead to a considerable gap between what is perceived as potentially available but is in no way affordable. The 'images' of the West may be consumed, but not necessarily the products. For example, few Muscovites can actually afford to eat at the McDonald's in Moscow.

4 (a) The Glasgow University Media Group claimed that through their research (for example into the British media coverage of the 1984/5 miners' strike) they found that the key pieces of information which audiences use to understand the world are themselves provided by the media.
A 'dominant media account' Philo et al. (1991) argue, is difficult to criticise without access to alternative sources of information. Hence, 54% of the GUMG's sample believed that most picketing was violent. Most of the people in the study did not use alternative information to 'negotiate' this 'dominant' message provided by the focus on the small number of instances by television and the press. Perhaps this 'bias' was not deliberately misleading because of the demand to print or broadcast what is considered editorially to be most 'newsworthy'. However, the resulting effect was to add weight to the argument of the government of the day and their policy on the use of 'flying pickets'.

   (b) The television news environment of today gives the appearance of greater objectivity through satellite technology providing instantaneous live access to events. However, this 'view' is still presented in a certain way and with information that gives the audience a particular view or slant on the image, even if it is live. Furthermore, political leaders and others have come to recognise the power of the immediacy of the message and, arguably, have learnt to manipulate it.

   (c) News in Britain could never be completely free from bias as the process of production of any news programme or publication inevitably involves some selection and prioritisation, i.e. what is left out and what is headline news could vary considerably between media and from day to day.

5 (a) For example, viewer (TV, cinema, video, billboard); listener (radio, music); consumer of music, literature, fashion, food and drink; part of a crowd (at a football match, rock concert or street demonstration). Think which ones of these are local, national or global audiences.

   (b) 'We' as a global audience are only informed to the extent that we are able to 'read' more than the dominant message on offer. For example, how reliant are we on a very narrow range of sources for our news?

6 (a) The deregulation of the airwaves introduced by the 1990 Broadcasting Act was largely welcomed from a New Right perspective and by those of a broadly liberal pluralist camp. However, concern from liberal paternalists would be in the form of an argument based on a decline in standards and in quality. With less regulation there is more freedom for broadcasters to appeal to the widest possible audience to ensure higher ratings and thus increased advertising and sponsorship revenues. However, that which appeals to the largest audience is not necessarily the 'highest quality' programming available.

   (b) Following the circumstances of the death of Diana, Princess of Wales, the role and freedom of the press was placed under a great deal of scrutiny. However, in Britain, a degree of self-censorship was declared by the press industry, aware of the potential damage to its image, and also to head off potential legislation to curb its freedom.

   (c) The advent of easy and relatively cheap electronic storage and instantly retrievable information, through computer databases, for example, allows organisations representing an issue or group to organise efficiently and quickly. Decisions made and announced by government, for example, can produce a very quick and organised response from those opposed to/affected by those decisions.
   For example, support for the defence of Louise Woodward was mobilised via the Internet in addition to the 'media circus' coverage of the case.
   How can a Marxist position explain developments in the new media with the apparent 'choice' available with the advent of the digital revolution? Cheap computers and relatively cheap access to the Internet increasingly allows access for the many, rather than the few.

7 With changing patterns of media ownership there is increased concern over regulation. Today, similar to other industries, a very few, very large companies have come to dominate the media world. Rupert Murdoch (News International), Ted Turner (CNN), and the late Robert Maxwell all can be classified as media moguls.

   Newspaper editors are inevitably responsive to the 'values' of their owners to some degree by virtue of the relationship of employer to employee. Ultimately though, it is circulation figures in relation to competitor titles which requires newspapers to provide content that sells. This, in turn, requires them to appeal to the social values of their readers, otherwise, presumably, readers would find it difficult to identify with the paper and thus not buy it.

   Does the political affiliation of readers and newspapers have an impact on this perspective?

Culture and identity

1   Is the distinction between 'high' and 'popular' culture still valid today (for example, consider the rise in affluence and the so-called new 'middle class')?

The increase in the prominence of the government department now known as 'Culture, Media and the Arts' perhaps indicates new priorities for 'popular' culture. For example, the government requiring that all national museums/galleries allow free admission 'for all', the funding of the National Lottery assisting a rejuvenation of theatre and the arts, the rise again in the popularity of cinema-going and football.

The deregulation of the airwaves in the 1990 Broadcasting Act was acclaimed as providing more choice in stations and channels – particularly with the advent of new digital technology. Are these genuine attempts to increase regional, minority and specialist programming, or merely a 'dumbing down' of culture where ultimately those programmes/stations/channels that provide the most popular entertainment in the commercial world (i.e. attract biggest audiences and sponsorship/advertising revenues) will come to dominate?

2   Cultural pluralists view the relationship between culture and society as largely positive. Audiences are active, and are active in the choices they make. Theirs is an informed consumption fulfilling genuine taste. The culture industries respond to the demand of the consumer rather than creating 'false' desires.

The neo-Marxist view loosely known as Critical Theory sees the 'culture industry' (after Adorno, 1944) as manipulative of mass markets. They claim there is a need to produce a critical analysis of the role of technology in the mass production of popular culture. This 'standardised' culture is imposed on the masses who uncritically accept it (passive audience and consumer). This is, in part, achieved through advertising which creates false needs and expectations on the part of the consumer. In this way, culture and the consumer get locked into the capitalist system.

3 The 'deterministic' view of cultural reproduction is that class culture is inevitably passed on from one generation to the next, with existing power relations built into this process.

Bourdieu uses the term 'symbolic violence' to describe the process of how everyone comes to be aware of 'reality' through culture, but at the same time are unaware of the continuance and reproduction of existing class relations as part of this same process.

Halsey provides a different emphasis from Bourdieu's cultural determinism, through looking at the role of material (physical and environmental) factors that influence educational attainment, which act in addition to cultural factors.

Abercrombie and Longhurst (1998) partly critique Bourdieu, claiming that 'developing patterns of taste and interaction which point to increased fluidity in taste are connected to the rise of the diffused audience and the patterns of distinction and classification within it'. Hence they paint a much less deterministic view of the nature of the relationship between culture and class. Rather, there seems to be developing 'new patterns of inclusion and exclusion'.

4 According to Ricoeur (1974) it is possible for the 'goals' of structuralism to be accomplished – to arrive at structure and science, but this comes at a great price that structuralists ignore. Namely, the researcher has to be working on 'a body of material which is preconstituted, stopped, closed, and in a certain sense, dead'. In this way there is no scope for understanding or meaning in context.

Geertz (1979) argues that meaning is given to action in the context of the larger cultural world: 'The art of interpretation is to make sense of context and world through attention to the means of interpretation members of a culture/society they themselves use'. So each culture and society contains its own interpretations. From this perspective the key is to learn how to gain access to these interpretations in order to understand them.

The weakness of structuralism from this perspective is its prescriptive and formalised nature which prevents the understanding of 'action, operations and process, all of which are constitutive of meaningful discourse' (Rabinow and Sullivan, 1979).

5   An apparent increased interest in the past has led to a rise in the number of museums and sites of historical interest, so much so that a whole industry has developed out of this, namely that of heritage (one way in which culture is commodified).

This can be seen as part of a search for a stable sense of local, national, or ethnic identity, in the roots of the tradition of a culture or society. Furthermore, post-modernism has an obsession with surface. The surface of style, 'selves', buildings, and places being more 'fluid' or changeable, though, does not necessarily mean the end of a stable identity 'within'. We routinely preserve a sense of our own history which forms our self-identity, a sense of 'who we are', through memorabilia, family photographs, and now camcorders have become a pervasive part of the way in which we form both individual and collective memories.

Family

1   (a) The apparent increased independence of the woman in the home in terms of her flexibility to work part-time, to shop at any time and the growth in the role of the 'third-party' carer (e.g. crèche or au pair) have contributed to other types of housework taking up more time. These increased expectations of provision of quality child-care and 'consumer choice' are not substitutes for routine domestic work but are mostly additional responsibilities. Although some research suggests a small degree of role-sharing of domestic labour, overall, the role of the man in the family has been much less affected, and he remains the key decision-making partner, i.e. transformations in the home have had little effect on power relationships.
    (b) So-called technological 'advances' have not reduced the time spent on domestic work. More, faster and more efficient appliances allowed the housewife to become more generalised in the duties she could perform. In this way technology can be said to shape the development of the family in terms of functions, as much as technology can be said to be responding to the 'needs' of the family.

2   Marxist accounts of the family which draw on factors such as class, time spent on housework, relations with children etc. are sometimes criticised as being 'gender-blind' for failing to focus on the structure of gender relations. They do not really consider housewives (Delphy and Leonard).

3   The fact that a high proportion of those partners who are divorced or separated seek a similar living arrangement tends to support the notion of the strength of the family in Britain. It may not be typically as long-lasting but the family has longevity as an ideal structure within which to raise children.

The 'failure' of marriage then is perceived by many as a fault in the relationship between partners rather than a poor reflection on the structure of 'the family' itself.

Furthermore, the notion of 'affective individualism' may contribute to a desire to seek fulfilment with a new partner. Hence, separation is not necessarily a reflection on the institution of the family itself.

4   (a) Lasch (1980), in his pessimism concerning American family life, does not really consider the notion of the 'reconstituted' family. Rather, he argues, 'It is clear . . . that the growing incidence of divorce, together with the ever-present possibility that any given marriage will end in collapse, adds to the instability of private life and deprives the child of a measure of emotional security'.

(b) The 'family unit' has traditionally been defined as opposite sex partners and at least one dependent child living together. If same sex partners are also included in this definition then clearly this implies the existence of some form of extended or additional family member or members. This is dependent on how the family came to be formed and whether one of the partners within the household is the natural father or mother of their dependent child or children.

5   Some commentators see the gentrification of the city (with its restoration of old houses) as developing new communities based on friendship. However, these areas tend to be fairly exclusive and for those who can afford to live in such areas.

Towns and cities are made up of numerous fragments of housing. The overall picture is much more diverse than traditional sociological accounts could have envisaged, with very different family experiences in different areas. Cities are increasingly cosmopolitan and affected by multiple factors including global influences.

Health

1   Health can be defined as biologically determined. The body is a machine that, when it malfunctions – as it naturally will – can be fixed through the use of medical technology.

    Alternatively good health can be seen as the norm, with ill-health being caused by social factors that impinge upon good health. These can include social class, geographical region, gender and ethnicity.

    Therefore both medical and social factors can be seen to affect health, but underlying them are different presumptions about whether good health or disease are the normal state of being. In your answer, try to explain which you consider to be more important, and why.

2   Lower income households have higher mortality (death) and morbidity (disease) rates. They also have a lower life expectancy, both at birth and at other times in life, and a higher infant mortality rate than higher-income families.

    Low income leads to poor diet and malnourishment, which can lead to disease.

    Poor quality and cramped housing conditions can cause disease and exacerbate its spread. For example, polluted water supplies and poor sanitation can lead to severe illness.

    Your answer should also consider any other effects of poverty. For example, are there any health effects linked to extreme wealth?

3   There is a distinct north–south regional health divide, with the majority of the lowest mortality- and morbidity-rate regions being in the south and the highest in the north.

    These tend, however, to correlate with higher and lower income, and thus class density, of these regions. For example Liverpool or Manchester have a high density of low socio-economic class households and a corresponding poor health record. By contrast Oxfordshire or Cambridgeshire have the opposite.

    Evidence for this can be seen from the high morbidity rates for East London, with its high density of low socio-economic class population. This is a southern region, but it shows high morbidity and mortality rates as a marker for low class and thus low income backgrounds, as do the northern regions.

4   Men and women are biologically different. They have different sexual and reproductive organs. Thus, by their physical biological differences they will be susceptible to different diseases; such as cancer of the breast in women and prostate cancer in men.

In addition to this, however, women and men are socialised differently. Smoking rates amongst men and women are different, both in terms of the percentage of the gender population smoking and the number and frequency of smoking. This will impact upon diseases such as lung cancer and heart disease.

The way in which men and women are socially constructed to deal with stress, men 'holding it in', women openly talking through their problems, will have a direct bearing on stress-related diseases such as heart disease. This is borne out in the statistics (Black Report, 1980), with men having higher heart disease morbidity and mortality rates.

Thus gender differences in health can be seen to be both biologically and socially constructed. What will be interesting is the way that changes in social construction of gender will affect the gendering of health in the next few decades.

5   Immigrants, particularly during the mass immigrations of the 1950s, tended to be healthier than the general population. This was despite poor domestic and working social conditions. It must, however, be remembered that immigration itself was a social screening mechanism for health. Those of poor health were unlikely to embark on the long, arduous and uncertain journey of emigration. Thus only those of very good health tended to be immigrants to Britain.

More recently the health of immigrants, particularly among second and third generation indigenously born members of ethnic families, has more closely reflected their socio-economic class within (British) society as a whole. There is now much evidence that conclusions to the contrary are based solely in racial stereotyping and pre-presumptions.

A further complication is the differential health of male and female immigrants. Thus it can be seen that ethnicity and health is a complex area which cannot show simple correlations with health and disease.

6   It is important to distinguish between mental disability (either from birth or through an event during a person's life, such as a head injury during a major fall or a car accident), and mental illness.

Mental disability is a substantial physical deformity or abnormality that precludes full mental functioning. Under the 1959 Mental Heath Act such a person would have been defined as 'subnormal'. More recently, the 1978 Warnock Report and the 1981 Education Act have defined such mental disability in terms of 'special needs' and the right to be assessed and provided with such requirements.

Mental illness, by contrast, is in its strictest medical sense a (temporary) state of mental being where 'normal' functioning is impaired or altered.

The problem with such a (medical) diagnosis of mental illness is the way in which such a labelling system is used. For example, as Rosenham (1978) showed, once labelled as schizophrenic patients continued to be described with this label even if they no longer showed symptoms of such mental illness, even over a substantial period of time. By the introduction of healthy 'patients', who initially faked symptoms of and were thus diagnosed as schizophrenic, he was able to show that once labelled, such people were stuck with the label of that illness, despite showing no further symptoms at all. There is therefore a tendency to diagnose illness rather than health, but unlike physical (as opposed to mental) disease such diagnosis is permanently socially imposed. This is a false positive diagnosis.

If doctors knew that such 'fake' patients might be being admitted at some point in the future (but in fact were not), they tended to under-diagnose compared to normal, despite the patient intake being unaltered. This is further evidence that mental illness is largely socially constructed.

By contrast, Foucault (*Madness and Civilization*) takes a non-judgemental historical retrospective of mental illness. In so doing he describes the way in which mental illness has been socially constructed in different societies at different times. He deliberately avoids definitions of 'madness', as what is or is not considered to be mad varies from period to period and society to society. Other cultures may have considered a person, that our own culture would consider to be mad, as someone who is possessed by spirits and therefore someone who has high social status because of their ability to foretell the future.

Thus mental health and illness can be seen to be heavily socially constructed and labelled as a state of being that has differed greatly at different times within our own social history and between different cultural constructions of mental health.

Education

1   The function of education is often constructed as a necessity in industrial societies technically, economically and socially. As education is the institutional centre for the transmission of learning, whoever is able to dictate what constitutes legitimate knowledge is in a position of power. Conversely, those excluded from the educational decision-making process are disenfranchised.

Conflict is largely 'built-in' to the more recent focus of debate within education on knowledge and teaching. For example, 'class' has been joined by race, gender and ethnicity in this respect. Sociological accounts are likely to focus more on education as a site of conflict, or rather as a site of a tangle of conflicts, in this period of 'late' or 'post-' modernity.

2   The rise in the numbers making up the so-called 'new' middle class is coupled with a rise in the educational aspirations of this group.

The expansion of higher education may be seen as an accommodation of this phenomenon, particularly with the conversion of many former polytechnic and other related institutions into 'new' universities during the 1990s.

3   Structuralist Marxists (Althusser, Bourdieu, Bowles and Gintis) argue education contributes to the socialising of lower-class groups into acceptance and conformity of a system that reinforces class inequality.

From this perspective, pupils are passive in their journey through the education system and into their destination of the lowest paid jobs. This approach does not explain, however, those pupils from lower-class backgrounds who do succeed academically. Fine (1991), for example, claims that her research shows the 'complicated, contradictory consciousness' operating within the minds and lives of poor and minority adolescents' (Wells, 1996). So structuralist Marxists do not adequately account for resistance, active agency and academic achievement amongst lower-class pupils.

4   With a very high percentage of pupils who take GCSE and A levels gaining high grades, this might increasingly be looked upon as a norm for attainment. 'Educational success' is perhaps viewed as a likely occurrence, thus the very few who do 'fail' in this system are more marginalised than they might have otherwise been, in today's reflexive media-informed environment of an 88% pass rate, for example.

5　Feminists might argue that females possess the potential to achieve as high, or indeed higher, than their male counterparts (as indicated by their performance at GCSE).

However, despite their success, girls are less likely to actually take A levels or go on to study in higher education (as reflected in the 1996 statistics).

Feminists contend that this is due to:

- sex-stereotyped 'vocational' subjects and courses encourage girls to follow career paths involving lower status, requiring lower qualifications and leading to lower rewards
- expanding service-sector (especially part-time and casual work) tends to 'fit in' with girls' traditional family commitments/roles (Weiner et al. 1997)
- the advent of a new gender discourse which has not celebrated the advances made by women but has instead emphasised male disadvantage. This is in part a 'backlash' against past feminist gains based on male fear of genuine equality.

Religion

1　The functionalist perspective would argue this case claiming that religion fulfils a fundamental need of society, that of integration. As traditional religions have declined, new forms of religious practice must arise, illustrations might be 'the cult of individualism' (see *Improve your knowledge*) and sport as religion (see below).

Marxism would also argue that religion will always change to meet the needs, not of society as a whole, but of the ruling group. We saw earlier how Methodism did this in the eighteenth century.

2　Typologies, or ideal types, are often used in sociology because:

- they allow for easy comparison of different and wide-ranging phenomena
- they allow us to see the essential aspects of various phenomena.

However, they do have certain drawbacks according to others:

- ideal types, or typologies, never actually exist
- the 'essential aspects' are not essential to the phenomenon but only to our definition of the phenomenon

- typologies lump together vastly different phenomena as if they were the same
- we ought to examine how religions are experienced by their members rather than impose characteristics.

3 **For**
- Formal religious practice (e.g. church attendance) has steadily declined this century.
- The institutional influence of the church has been in decline over several centuries.

Against
- Religion has changed its form, becoming more personalised and consumer oriented.
- There has been a growth in new religious movements.
- There has been a growth of world religions in Britain.
- The secularisation thesis only seems to work in certain parts of the world, namely Europe. As Europe and the West has declined, so world religions have become more powerful as a local response to globalisation.

4 Durkheim's work was anthropological, which meant that when he was studying religion he was seeing how it fitted into a whole cultural system. In this it did so, as all members of the clans played a part in the rituals and festivals. Because of this the rituals reinforced the conscience collective of the culture on a face-to-face level.

However, modern society is not face-to-face in the same way, so either religion has to work at a different level, or integration must be performed by other institutions. Parsons attempted to apply Durkheim's analysis to modern society, arguing that religion is a specialist institution focusing on its specific tasks. This is one possible way of using Durkheim's theory in a modern setting. Another way is to see everyday interaction rituals as being part of the 'cult of individualism' and arguing, as Randall Collins does, that Durkheim's theory still works – it is just that we must explore it at a different level relevant for modern societies.

5 Secularisation was part of the modernist 'grand narratives' of liberalism and Marxism. With the relativisation of the West due to globalisation, post-modernism is the dawning on the West that it cannot order the world as it sees fit. Hence a post-modern 'world', i.e. the West, is one in which religions play a major part in many areas of the globe politically, culturally and economically. Moreover, given the declining belief in any 'grand narrative' within the West, it has become permissible to utilise religions and religious techniques and practices for one's own fulfilment; religion in the post-modern West is becoming increasingly a 'lifestyle choice' for many.

6 Using a broad definition of religion we can see sport as a religion. For like religion,

- sport shapes and reinforces central values in society
- sports events are (national) community rituals
- celebrating sports is like worshipping
- sports provide intense excitement and a spirit of community
- football grounds, like churches, are sacred spaces, e.g. Wembley's 'hallowed' turf
- sport has saints and gods.

7 Ideology – a set of ideas, beliefs and values which serves to justify and naturalise the subordination of one group by another. The ruling classes, whose ideas in any age are the ruling ideas, use religion as a means of propagating their ideology and so producing a 'false class consciousness' among the proletariat. Religion justifies the interests of the bourgeoisie because it reflects the economic mode of production. It is a way of explaining and so justifying why things are the way they are.

Power and politics

1 Marxist theory consists of a powerful model but it is relatively 'fixed' and more difficult to adapt to suit requirements – you have to accept the central tenets of the theory in order to use it.

Weber's concepts are less powerful as an explanation but are not so complete and therefore easier to mould to or around a given position.

Weber considers skills/qualifications as a major basis of class, whereas Marxists have a problem in explaining the growth of the middle class who do not own the means of production and the possibility of them developing a 'false class consciousness'.

2   Consider the changing nature of the state of our democracy: the moves underway towards a claimed 'decentralisation' or 'devolvement' of power to regional parliaments/assemblies. Also:

- the role and independence of the civil service and debates over access to government
- ownership and control of the mass media and the Murdoch–'New Labour' relationship
- instances of the use of force to uphold the rule of law, e.g. Northern Ireland marches, inner-city riots, and trade union disputes of the 1980s.

3   The changing nature of institutions – the privatisation of industries with the appointment of very well paid heads; the new system of NHS Trust Management introduced by the Conservative government.

4   Consider the change in the nature of the working class itself (decline in 'traditional' working-class employment with deindustrialisation, increased affluence, Right to Buy legislation, mobility etc.) and the process of class dealignment.

Voters tend to support the party they see as best representing their own interests, thus voting along issue lines and the 'feel-good factor', rather than old class divides.

Labour's 'reinvention' as 'New Labour' was founded upon the work done by Neil Kinnock as leader in tackling the militant (far Left) tendencies, following the defeat of Michael Foot in 1983.

5   Each party has its strengths and weaknesses in terms of public popularity of different issues. In 1992 the dominant issue covered by TV was 'the economy', which was considered as a strength of the Conservatives, whereas voters mistrusted Labour on this issue. In 1997, however, 'Europe' dominated coverage, on which the Conservatives were perceived as being fundamentally split, and 'the economy' had slipped to the eighth most covered issue by TV. Thus, these could have been contributory factors to the Conservative win of 1992 and Labour's of 1997.

Negative images (of division, sleaze and scandal) might be considered as more **newsworthy** (in terms of audience/readership figures) than positive news (e.g. of policy).

By highlighting issues/stories such as the Neil Hamilton affair and the personal conduct of MPs, other issues of broader political concern, and each party's position on them, are not covered and debated to such an extent. Thus, it can be argued that the public are less well informed on party/government policy in a media environment that affects the political process (what is prioritised) in a climate where newsworthiness increasingly influences media headlines and thus politicians' reactions.

Theory and methods

1 The main criticisms are outlined below.

- Quantitative methods give a researcher little or no insight into the meanings or motives upon which social action is based.
- Quantitative methods involve the imposition of a researcher's own categories onto the meanings of people's actions.
- Far from being 'objective', quantitative data require subjective interpretation anyway, both at the level of categorisation and the level of pattern-reading.
- As such, a source such as official statistics simply reflects the categories and preconceptions of their author.
- People who advocate quantitative methods seldom adhere to their own suggested methodologies. When attempting to explain the suicide rates in different areas, for example, Durkheim began to speculate upon individuals' subjective states.

2 *Verstehen* is Max Weber's notion of 'understanding'. He suggested that before any explanations of social action can be posited it is necessary to directly observe, interpret and understand the motivations and meanings for any given social action, as they are for an actor him- or herself in actual real-world cases, rather than to simply assume set meanings for set actions. He suggested that from this point, connections and causal relations could then be generated.

- Symbolic interactionists likewise are concerned with the explanation of social actions and the meanings that people give to them. Like Weber, the symbolic interactionists' view is that it is necessary to focus on specific instances of action and interaction. Unlike Weber, however, the work of Mead, Blumer and Goffman tends to resist generalising its findings to a macrosocial level and avoids talking of 'large scale social change'. Much of their work takes the form of very specific case studies.

- Ethnomethodologists go further still. While their focus remains upon the meanings formed by people in their everyday actions and interactions, and the practical element of their work involves direct empirical observation and interpretation, they resist positing any explanations at all, arguing that the best anybody can do when explaining is speculate. They thus stick to two primary principles: Description rather than explanation, and Indifference, that is they make no value judgements and resist theorising of all kinds, addressing only highly specific instances of action.

3   Gouldner is arguing against Durkheim, who believes that sociology can be scientific, objective and value-free at all levels, and against Weber who argues that although sociology cannot be value-free at the level of topic selection, sociologists should resist making explicit value-judgements or statements of bias in their work. As such he is also arguing against the stands of Symbolic Interactionism and, particularly, Ethnomethodology.

The primary problem with his argument is that if a sociologist cannot choose a topic or carry out research without being affected by the influence of values, then he or she can hardly be expected to perform self-analysis without the same constraints. Thus, any statement regarding the values of the researcher can be as potentially distorted, biased and misleading as his or her research. If one is to accept that values affect all judgements, then explicit statements of one's own personal bias are hardly necessary or helpful. As C. Wright Mills once claimed, ' . . . the reasons that men give are not themselves without reasons . . . '. If one is to start giving reasons for why one's research is 'like it is', then one must start looking for reasons for the reasons, and reasons for the reasons for the reasons and so on in an infinite regress. Ethnomethodologists, for example, preserve an indifference in their own work, but sporadically also turn their own analyses of meanings and methods back onto themselves as a reminder that they are not claiming 'objectivity' or 'neutrality' (embedded in their creeds are the notions that nothing is objective or neutral). They are, rather, avoiding drawing grand conclusions from small pieces of evidence to minimise the influence of their own values.

4   Very broadly, Functionalism and Classical Marxism both view societies as social 'wholes', as systems, and both view that these systems can be analysed on a 'macro' level from an external perspective using 'scientific' techniques.

- They are both, thus, structuralist.
- Both view that individual behaviour is determined primarily by wider

social factors. Parsons, for example, views the whole as a harmonious unit which is necessarily like it is in order to function at all.

- Marx, however, views that the 'whole' is seriously divided into class factions and only held together by the exercise of unjust power.
- Furthermore, while functionalists view that the primary determinants of social behaviour are a shared consciousness (Durkheim) or culture (Parsons), Marxists view that the prime determinants are economic (Marx) and ideological (Gramsci).
- As such, Functionalism stresses co-operation between different groups in society, while Marxism stresses conflict.
- Both Functionalism and Marxism have been accused of 'social determinism'.

5 Bryman is referring to the way in which qualitative and quantitative methods have become almost religiously the territory of social action and structural perspectives respectively. Social action theorists defend the use of qualitative techniques because they are crucial to their whole social approach, while structuralists defend quantitative methods for the same reasons. In either case, to criticise the methodology is to criticise everything about the theories and theorists. Bryman's point is that this is a relatively artificial argument because virtually all researchers have at one point or another (notably Weber) used combinations of methods. He advocates this methodological pluralism as it can allow the researcher to 'triangulate' data. Triangulation is useful because:

- the accuracy of a conclusion can be checked by examining it in the light of both quantitative and qualitative data
- hypotheses can be generated from qualitative data which can subsequently be explored quantitatively
- more complete pictures of a given social group can be generated from the conjoining of the two types of methodology
- qualitative data and research can be used to justify the statistical correlation of certain variables.

6 In highly simplified terms, Sociology is the study of society and social phenomena using a number of techniques, while Social Policy is the pragmatic implication of social theories and ideologies (usually as based on the conclusions from given research) on a legislative basis with a view to altering or preserving social conditions. As such, Sociology can also involve the study of social policy and its effects.